3. 60

JOURNEY TO PEKING

為中美攜手達
「三世界永久和平。」
題念存

譚平先生

陳香文
敬書荃。

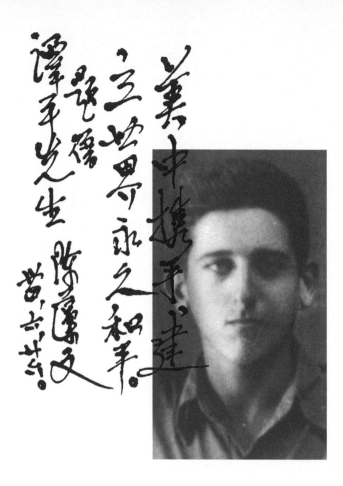

JOURNEY to PEKING

A SECRET AGENT IN WARTIME CHINA

DAN PINCK

Naval Institute Press

Annapolis, Maryland

Naval Institute Press
291 Wood Road
Annapolis, MD 21402

Library of Congress Cataloging-in-Publication Data
Pinck, Dan C.
    Journey to Peking : a secret agent in wartime China / Dan Pinck.
    p. cm.
    ISBN 1-59114-677-1 (alk. paper)
    1. Pinck, Dan C. 2. United States. Office of Strategic Services.
3. World War, 1939–1945—Secret service—United States. 4. World
War, 1939–1945—China. 5. World War, 1939–1945—Personal
narratives, American. I. Title.
    D810.S8 P465 2003
    940.54'8673'092—dc21

                                                    200201421

Printed in the United States of America on acid-free paper ♾
10 09 08 07 06 05 04 03   9 8 7 6 5 4 3 2
First printing

This book is for Joan Pinck.

Lost in you I find,
welcome places in my mind.

CONTENTS

PREFACE

In the fall of 1986, I attended a two-day reunion of Office of Strategic Services (OSS) veterans at the Mayflower Hotel in Washington, D.C. Several people who later served as directors of the Central Intelligence Agency, the successor to the wartime OSS, relived their OSS adventures and exchanged stories with about eighty men and women. Then–CIA director William J. Casey, former directors William E. Colby and Richard Helms, and a former CIA deputy director, Ray S. Cline, told us their stories and we told them ours. Since no former OSS agent present had shared experiences with anyone else during the war, no one could dispute anyone's recollections. I claimed to have been one of the youngest, if not the youngest, major general during World War II. No one doubted me. Some of the other stories were even more outlandish. I accepted everyone's history as they accepted mine.

A reporter from the *New York Times* covered the reunion. The next day, a prominent news story about it was published in the *Times*, and my recollections were a significant part of the story:

Dan Pinck, then just 18, brought with him to the OSS a Boy Scout handbook that a neighbor in Bethesda, Maryland, had assured him would be helpful anywhere.

"I was given millions of dollars and a crate of condoms to give to Chinese leaders," he said. "I didn't even know what they were for."

He was also told to send back a map showing Japanese emplacements in a Chinese town, but he didn't know how to draw a map, so he turned to the Scout manual. Using a section called "Getting to Mrs. Nestor's Farm," Mr. Pinck carried out his order.

On the plane back to Boston, my wife, Joan, said about the reunion, "I've never heard such flapdoodle in my life."

Our youngest son, Charlie, met us at Logan Airport. He looked at me rather quizzically and didn't say much. He and Joan talked to each other while I collected our bags. Shortly after we arrived home, Joan said to me as we began unpacking, "Charlie read the *New York Times.* Do you know what he asked me?" she said. "No," I said. "I haven't the slightest idea. What did he say?" Joan said, "Charlie wanted to know if it was true that you didn't know what a condom was." I said, "Of course I knew what a condom was. But I'd never seen one before." Joan said, "Well, you'd better talk to him."

When our three other children called to find out the answer to the same question, I knew I had some explaining to do. "They don't know what you did during the war or if anything you've told them about it—which is not much—is true," Joan said. "You've got a problem."

A year or two later, I wrote an article about my experiences in China that was published in *Encounter.* I gave copies of it to my children, Tony, Jenny, Alexandra, and Charlie.

They liked it and I felt as though I was off the hook: no more condom comments.

Before that I had published snippets of my China experiences in various publications, including the *Boston Globe*. And, after my *Encounter* article, I mentioned China in an article in the *American Scholar* and *Financial Times*. The *American Scholar* piece was about A. J. Liebling, for whom I served as a legman for two years. He wrote splendid articles about his experiences during World War II in England, Europe, and North Africa, and he and I enjoyed swapping war stories.

Perhaps it was my rereading Liebling that moved me to write this book about my war in China. That and putting my boxes of war memorabilia in order: messages I sent encoded on one-time pads to headquarters, messages I received and decoded, copies of letters and official correspondence with Chinese colleagues, testimonials I received when the war was over, photographs and maps, and, surprisingly, notes I made during the war about some of my experiences. Twice I was ordered by headquarters to destroy all of my possessions, except for my armament, when they considered that I was in danger of being captured by the Japanese. Of course, I destroyed nothing.

War books that I am most fond of are those that move along unheroically and with a quixotic imperturbability, no matter how desperate the situation. They are accounts of reasonable young men in a series of unreasonable situations. War itself is seldom absent, but its emotional dimension is often mitigated by the writer's refusal to take himself too seriously.

Some of these books are Siegfried Sassoon's *Memoirs of an Infantry Officer*, John Verney's *Going to the Wars*, Laurie Lee's *Moment of War*, Robert Graves's *Goodbye to All That*, Samuel

Hynes's *Flights of Passage*, Desmond Bristow's *Game of Moles*, David Smiley's *Albanian Assignment*, John Mulgan's *Report on Experience*, A. J. Liebling's *Normandy Revisited* (he ate well between battles), George MacDonald Fraser's *Quartered Safe Out Here*, and Jack Hemingway's *Misadventures of a Fly Fisherman* (as the OSS member of a Jedburgh team, he parachuted into France with a fishing rod in his kit). Add a jigger of Evelyn Waugh's trilogy, *Men at Arms, Officers and Gentlemen,* and *Sword of Honor,* and you know the bent of my mind.

I was certain that I wouldn't be captured. Sometimes you guess right. War is like that.

JOURNEY TO PEKING

A SMALL CORNER
OF THE WAR

THE WAR did not exist in Hotien, a tired hill town about 120 kilometers up the coast from Hong Kong and inland a rough 30. The base of our operations in the Office of Strategic Services, Hotien ran about three hundred yards along a dirt pathway from the high mud wall of the school at the north entrance to the crumbling sentry tower standing guard on the path to the sea. Four hundred people, perhaps not that many, made up the population. Daily their brown feet joggled about the village, coolies burdened with caddies of rice, storekeepers tipping their short-brimmed felt hats at each other, guerrillas dressed only in coolie-blue shorts, carrying single Czechoslovakian hand grenades that resembled bowling pins.

The guerrillas, numbering about two hundred, were under the command of General Tong. They had orders from the generalissimo not to annoy the Japanese. "Do not fire on Nips," he ordered. "They will take revenge by killing our women and children. Wait." The guerrillas waited and cursed and smiled. Every harvest time, and even more often than that, the Japanese would come inland from their garrison in the sea town in small groups and forage for a few days in the river valley near Hotien. On their return to the garrison, they would bring back rice and pigs and women. Although when the rice harvest was small or had been well hidden by the farmers, the Japanese would replace the rice with women and they would eat and rape on their way back to the sea town. General Tong would notify us by courier when the Japanese were in the river valley and we would take to the hills. After the enemy left, we would return to Hotien and have a party, get drunk on rice wine and Hong Kong aerated water, and toast our victory over the Japanese.

I had volunteered to serve behind Japanese lines, to gather and transmit intelligence about Japanese troop movements inland and along the South China coast. As an agent of the Office of Strategic Services, I was now the nearest American to Hong Kong. Armed with several million dollars in Chinese money, kept in two large straw suitcases under my slat bed in the Chinese Roman Catholic mission in Hotien, my interpreter Shum and I would close the door and the windows every few days, remove one of the suitcases and open it, and take out forty or fifty thousand dollars without accurately counting it. Then we would stuff the money in our pockets, open the door, and wait for our Chinese agents to come in from the coastal towns to give us information about Japanese movements. For the information, we would give each agent about four thousand dollars. Usually we had about twenty agents working for us.

I didn't know much about intelligence. Neither did I know the Chinese language. I was ready to sit out the war behind the lines, far from Army regulations and the stupid boredom of the war in western China, but I wanted to be a hero, on my own terms, in my own fashion. It had taken me about two years to forget that I had been a student at Washington and Lee University, struggling with introductory physics, Victorian literature, and required gym three days a week, before I joined the Army. I had been determined to go on active duty and to avoid joining an Army or Navy reserve program; some of my friends were still in college under such programs. I wanted to fight. I wanted to win medals. I wanted a Purple Heart. I wanted not to be bored. After I joined the Army, I wanted to get as far away as possible from the Army, from subordination as well as command. I wanted to be exactly where I was, in China, away from the rule book of war yet immersed in a special kind of war. I could become a hero and not accept any medals. I could become a silent hero and tightly guard any distortions of the truth. If I wanted to, I could conceal myself at parade rest and pretend that my emotions were at half-mast; I might slide through the war, awake or not to the impressions and decisions that would make *my* mission a successful one. I wanted most to collect impressions and avoid displays of authority. I was determined to be a reasonable young intelligence agent, removed from unreasonable military situations. Molehills do become mountains when we treat them that way. China was a small corner of the war; and my corner, I hoped, would be an end in itself.

I did not care to stand up and be committed for any other kind of adventure.

I wanted to be adroit and fearless, on my own terms. "Don't take any risks," my father had told me before I left home on my last leave, "and don't volunteer for anything. I was in the Army in the first World War and I know. Listen to me." Dad survived his war; I didn't believe he had followed his advice at any time. When I was six years old, he had given me his collection of medals to keep in my room. He played heads and tails with them whenever I showed them to him, never telling me exactly what he did to get them.

My OSS training had not occurred in a former country club in the suburbs of Washington; it had taken place not long ago, in China, in Hingning. Hingning was a refugee-crowded city to which I had first come after a three days' walk from a secret airfield behind Japanese lines. It was a pinched city, its streets were its seams, and poorly clad people walking hurriedly sprawled in mosaic colors on the dirt roads leading to the countryside. Penny-colored brassware hung at different heights from wooden pegs in shops and embrasures. Bordering the country roads, bamboos kept time with the winds; when the breezes came into town, they ruffled linen and cotton cloths hanging in the backs of shops. The tea shops, which served more than just tea, did a fine business, and occasionally you would meet soldiers staggering down the street, holding bottles of rice wine. The war was some other place.

Maj. Lucas Fletcher, who before the war had been a sales agent for the British and American Tobacco Company in China, was in charge of OSS operations in Southeast China.

He and five American assistants lived in a walled compound just outside of Hingning. Major Fletcher briefed me: my chief concerns were to be the gathering and transmission of intelligence and meteorological data, knowing when the Japanese got too close, knowing when to give a party to obtain close cooperation, and, finally, how to make contacts for my own business ventures in China after the war.

"You'll meet generals," the major told me one morning. "They are not really so important. To them, you'll be much more important than they really are to you."

I nodded.

"If you make a good impression, Pinck, they might be able to get you into business here after the war. Export, import. Lots of money in it. What the hell?" He answered himself before I had time to speak. "By God, I wish I were in your shoes!" he bellowed.

I nodded.

"What the hell, I've got a good deal here," he said.

"Yessir," I said, trying to match the tone of my voice to his.

"You are a representative of the United States. The success of your mission depends on whether the Chinese like you. Remember first impressions are the last impressions here." He paused a moment and ran his hands through his hair. "Close cooperation," he continued. "That's it."

This was the nature of one morning's briefing. Until he could find an interpreter and a radio operator for me, I was able to take it easy in the compound or in the town and attend briefings in the morning.

Not long after this session, Fletcher called me into his

office. He was examining a hole in his khaki shirt when I arrived. He looked up and said, "You'd better take a couple dozen pro-kits with you."

In Kunming, I told him, I had signed for iodine, sulfadiazine, and grosses of pro-kits. OSS headquarters in Kunming said that these were to be my medical supplies.

"Give some to the Chinese," he said. "Hard to get good ones out here, and they like them. One old general wanted me to form a contraceptive and cesspool company with him after the war. I told him no. I've already got my oil. But maybe you can run into a deal like that."

I nodded.

"You'll need those things out there." He grinned. "You'll take to wine or women. Probably both. You'll go crazy if you don't. You'll go crazy if you do."

And that was the end of that briefing.

One day Fletcher called me into his office and introduced me to a slim, intense young man. "This is Shum Hay," he said. "He's going to be your interpreter."

We shook hands. A nice looking fellow, I thought.

"My name's Dan Pinck," I said.

"Ich bin freulich Sie sind hier," he said.

What the hell is this? I wondered.

The major raised his hand wearily and said, "Nein, Shum." He looked severely at the young Chinese man. "That will never do." Major Fletcher turned to me. "Shum was a medical student in Meishan when I interviewed him for this job. His teachers were Germans. Shum knows German better than he knows English." Then he turned to Shum and said, "Speak English, Shum."

"Righto," said Shum.

The major got tired suddenly and told us to work it out for ourselves. We thanked him and left his office. Outside, I said, more or less to myself, "This is a crock."

"Do not know *crock*," said Shum.

I said again, louder, "This is a crock."

"Do not know *crock*," he said flatly and so scornfully that I felt he must know the innuendos which can be inherent in the tone of the English language.

I smiled stupidly.

"When you say word I do not know, I say 'do not know' word you say," he said.

"Oh?"

"Yes."

"Yes."

"Give me practice," said Shum.

"You aren't overburdened with crudition," I told him.

"Do not know *overburdened*. Do not know *erudition*. You practice me," he said happily.

Over the next days, I practiced Shum in English. Then I was jolted to learn that our radio operator, who was introduced to us soon after, knew English very well. His name was Lung Chui Wah. "My English not so good," he said when we met him. "Forget I know English. Too much work for me if I know English. I think never mind. Just operate radio. Do not speak English." Lung's chin came down to a small insignificant flattened squareness, as though an artist in making a papier-mâché mask had run out of paper near the chin. "You understand?" he asked me. "Best cooperation that way."

We left Hingning in the early morning after a monsoon

week. Fletcher drove us on a winding road through pine trees and over streams to a river, about twenty kilos from Hingning. The weather was cool, the wind blowing inland from the sea. As we turned off a high hill road down to the river, we saw Hingning disappear in a valley of paddy fields. At the river Shum hired a sampan. Major Fletcher seemed to be relieved when we were ready to push off downstream. He took out a bottle of Four Roses, drank some, and gave the bottle to me. "Drink," he said ominously, as though he expected me to be fully aware that I might not return, and that this might be my last drink of Four Roses on this earth. I drank and then gave the bottle to Shum. "Drink," I said. Shum said nothing; he smelled the contents and quickly gave the bottle to Lung. "Damn good," said Lung, after drinking a lot. He gave the bottle to the major, and we stepped from the riverbank onto the sampan. The polers began their labor, trying to put us out in the main current, and the boat moved slowly from the riverbank. Shum, Lung, and I stood between two small suitcases at the stern, one full of pro-kits, the other packed with Chinese money. The major waved to us and we waved to him. As soon as he emptied the bottle, he threw it far out in the river and left. We were on our own.

Shum kept a record of our expenses during the trip. Not that it was necessary to keep a statement of expenses (the OSS had undisclosed amounts for undisclosed purposes), but I was curious to know how we spent our money, for a week or so at least. Keeping a record was, besides, good language practice for Shum. We spent $27,051 on our river journey:

Date	Particular	Expense
15 April	sampan from Sui Mau to Sui Chai	$5,000
	tiffin	$4,000
	supper	$6,220
16 April	steamboat from Sui Chai to Han Lu	$9,000
	breakfast	$275
	supper	$818
	five coolies from Hen Lu to Colonel An's house	$1,500
	tea for coolies	$238
	TOTAL	$27,051

We were all rather happy over the suitcase full of money. The suitcase reminded me of the never-empty pitcher of wine which belonged to Greek mythology's Philemon and Baucis. The money would not only impress others, including any Chinese businessmen-in-the Army we might meet, but, more immediately, it gave us confidence in our ability to meet any-one on our side of the war and successfully gain close coop-eration. We made a solemn pact, in three languages, before we reached our destination on the river. Shum made his in German, for he said that a pact made in German could never be broken. Our wishes were that we would have good luck and that we would kill many Japanese with our intelligence (which would reach the Fourteenth Air Force). Shum said that he was sure the Chinese would like us and give us "a close cooperation." I was a friend of his bosom, he said. Lung said I was a damn good friend.

It was dusk when we reached Hen Lu, and we went immediately to Colonel An's house, where we would spend the night before starting our overland trip to Hotien. After a frugal dinner of rice and soybeans, a number of military and civilian officials came to the house for a conference. They told us how best to proceed in the hills and how to avoid the Japanese along the coast. They wanted to know how the war was going in Europe and when we would invade Japan. A civilian asked me whether President Roosevelt liked the Chinese people. I assured him that, yes, Roosevelt liked the Chinese people; in fact, he liked them more than any other of our allies in the war. The civilian smiled, shook my hand, and said that he had heard that Roosevelt had many Chinese friends. I said he had many Chinese friends. Colonel An and Shum talked a few minutes. I was silent.

"The colonel says," said Shum, the fulcrum of our verbal seesaw, "it's best for us to sleep here in his house and do not travel at night. No one travels at night in China. We need sleep. Shall I tell the colonel that we are happy to sleep in Hen Lu? Best safety."

"Okay," I said.

Then we drank a cup of tea in honor of the Air Force. Shum spoke again to the colonel.

"Colonel An says he thinks we better travel by bicycle tomorrow, and not walk," Shum said.

"Okay," I said.

Every now and then, I noticed to my bewilderment that the Chinese grimaced after I answered Shum. And after my last "okay," Colonel An spit out his tea.

Shum nudged me. "We go outside," he said nervously.

"Okay," I answered, wondering what was up.

He stood up, bowed, and excused us; then he took my

elbow and led me to a wooden balcony outside the dining room.

"Not all right to say 'okay' so often," he said.

What the hell? I wondered.

"'Okay' very bad," he added.

"What the hell, Shum, 'okay' means all right."

"In Cantonese, 'okay' means shit."

"Do not say word any more," he cautioned, leading me by my elbow back into the dining room. I sat stupefied as the Chinese talked on and on, and when they wanted an answer from me, I merely nodded my head. When the conference ended and the Chinese were leaving the room in small groups, I said, "What the hell," fearing that my chances of ever obtaining close cooperation with these men were practically nil, and that my chances of being invited to form a contraceptive and cesspool company after the war were pretty dim.

Shum told me much about himself and his life in Hong Kong before the war. In Hong Kong his life had centered on the hasty dispatching of any ideas and actions inimical to those of their British protectors. To be subservient but never humble, pleasant but never unctuous had been taught to Shum by his father, who occupied an official position in the Hong Kong government. Shum's manners were pleasant, his carriage slim but sturdy. He moved with an ease of self-confidence which, he told me proudly, gave his father grave concern for his welfare. His father, Shum said, was an unimaginative man of the patience-is-a-lovely-virtue school. Shum said he molded his own actions between compromise and moderation, and, as a converted Christian, he owned an

enthusiasm which, he hoped, would not be thought pre-
sumptuous by his non-Christian friends: he had a passion for
religion and the good way of life. A philosophy teacher of
his in Hong Kong had converted him to the Protestant faith,
and like most converts, Shum's devotion was greater than
that of those born into a religion. Buddhism remained the
faith of his father. Shum said that he and his father during
their days in Hong Kong would, upon the slightest provoca-
tion, invoke the didacticisms of their two religions and carry
on chapter-long warfare until both of them had forgotten the
point of the original dispute. But Shum was able to get along
with his father with a necessary amount of filial respect. To
censure, to pass judgment, to condemn, and, finally, to forgive
—such was the circuitous method, he said, of the righteous,
who judge themselves by the same stern standards by which
they judge others. Shum said that he would go so far as to die
for his religion; he couldn't see anyone dying for Buddha.

On the last day of our trip, I asked him where he thought
we ought to stay in Hotien.

"The Catholic mission is the best place for safety," he said
diffidently. "It is always. In the insides of China it is like
Middle Ages in Europe. Missions are like hotels."

I suggested maybe we would have good food at the
mission.

"No good food," he said glumly. "Chinese food."

Then I suggested that we would be safest there; we would
live through the end of the war.

"I hope so," Shum said. "That would make me pleasure."

It was late afternoon of the third day of our overland
journey when we first saw Hotien. The color of evening was

brushing the sides of the mountains into chalk-gray and purple and coursing down the valley into Hotien. Threads of house smoke wound upward into a cloud of haze above the town. Soon we reached the Catholic mission. Built outside the town, the mission was encircled by a winding wall. We went to a small enclosure inside the wall and met the priest; smiling, his arms akimbo, he spoke to Shum for a few minutes. Tall shoots of bamboo were sentinels around the enclosure.

When the priest finished, Shum said, "The priest is called Father Tan. He says that he has gladness to see us, and asks us to forgive this garden in which we are standing. Nothing much grows. Father Tan says the fertilizer consists of prayers; they take a while."

The priest smiled and shook our hands, then he led us past the thick walnut door of the mission house and into the center courtyard. Faded maps of China and the world hung on the cement walls around the courtyard, and above the maps of China were pictures of Generalissimo Chiang Kai-shek, the president of China, staring moodily. Naked children were having fun in the courtyard, flicking water at one another from wooden buckets. Shadows moved all over the yard, and a patch of light was growing smaller on the wall nearest the highest picture of the generalissimo. There couldn't be a war going on near this place, I felt. At least not at this time of the day.

Father Tan and Shum talked to each other for several minutes before Shum said to me, "The shinfoo says we must not hate Japs. I told him we don't hate them but we want to kill them."

I asked Shum the meaning of *shinfoo*; he told me it was Chinese for "priest." I could call him, Shum said, the shinfoo, the priest, or Father Tan.

Shum spoke to Father Tan.

"The shinfoo says," said Shum, "that the Japs are near us, but we will know before they come to Hotien, so we will have good time to go to the hills."

Father Tan went away through one of the doorways, and when he returned, moving in a pontifical shuffle, he carried a dusty bottle and four cups on a green-brass tray. He threw water from a wooden bucket on a couple of children and laughed; he put the wooden bucket upside down on the cement floor and placed the tray upon it.

"Shum," I said, looking at Father Tan, "you tell the priest that he has a big chance to help us win the war. Tell him that we would like to live in his mission, that it will hasten the end of the war."

Shum looked impatient. "Is that all?" he asked.

I nodded for him to go ahead.

He began talking to Father Tan, whose hands were hidden in the bloomerlike folds of his sleeves. Shum seemed to be using his hands as a verbal aid, flopping them down or flinging them to the side in swift gestures denoting urgency, appeal, necessity.

Then Shum turned to me and said dejectedly, "He says his house a Catholic mission, only opens for religion. The shinfoo say he hopes the war ends soon."

"Tell him," I said, "that we wish it too. If he lets us stay here the war may be over sooner."

"The shinfoo says no soldiers stay in Catholic mission.

On the wall under that picture of Chiang Kai-shek are orders from him not to let soldiers stay in Catholic missions."

"Ask him why, Shum."

"The shinfoo says it is because soldiers are not considerate of property. Soldiers have camped in mission compounds and they built fires. The shinfoo says when there is no wood from trees and sticks, soldiers take beams from mission houses. Also chairs. The shinfoo says he does not like soldiers."

"Tell him we don't either."

Shum shook his head and said, "The shinfoo asks why we are soldiers."

"We want to drive the Japanese out of China."

"The shinfoo says God does not like soldiers."

"Tell Father Tan that God does not like Japs."

"He says God does."

Shum was obviously losing enthusiasm for the conversation. For a moment, I thought that Lung, perhaps, might be able to gain Father Tan's favor, but, I noticed to my consternation, Lung had poured himself a cup of wine without having been offered any. And Father Tan was looking at him, sadly surveying him from head to foot.

"Hell, Shum," I said with a hopeless feeling, "tell him we don't like soldiers. We hate all soldiers."

"The shinfoo says we must not hate, and wants to know why we are soldiers."

"God wants us to be soldiers."

"He says God wants no one to be soldiers."

"Tell him we are soldiers because we want to make him free."

"The shinfoo says he is free. He says, 'Have no fear, Jesus Christ will protect us.'"

We did not answer.

"The shinfoo says war will end in good time." Shum wiped his forehead with a handkerchief.

"Tell him that Chiang Kai-shek and Franklin D. Roosevelt wish us to stay in his mission at Hotien."

"The shinfoo says he would say the same to them," Shum said emphatically.

Father Tan rolled up his sleeves, showing thick, strong arms, much too heavy for his size. He bowed to Shum and spoke to him in Chinese. Shum's white shirt was watery with perspiration; he held his shirt out from his chest and blew down under it, making long whistling sounds. Father Tan stopped abruptly.

"It puzzles me," said Shum, blowing harder. "You let me do talking and we will see."

I told him to go ahead and talk. After a few minutes, he stopped talking to Father Tan and said, "He says what religion are we. I tell him one of us is Catholic, maybe he will let us stay. He wants to know which one." Shum and I looked at Lung.

"No," said Lung. "I know nothing. Do not know mass."

"You be Catholic," Shum said to me. "You need religion most."

"No, not me," I said.

"I know," Shum said suddenly. "We will play pull-the-longest. Get straws or matches. One who pulls the longest is Catholic."

Lung looked at me; I looked at Lung; we two nodded to Shum that it was a good idea. Shum took a matchbox from his trousers pocket and, facing us, so that the enterprise was hidden from the sight of Father Tan, removed three matches from it. He broke the matches into different sizes, made a fist, and stuck the matches in it. "Pull," he said. I pulled one; it seemed fairly short. Then Lung pulled one, and his seemed to be short. "No need for me to pull," Shum said. "I am it." He turned around and started talking to Father Tan.

"The shinfoo says it is nice night tonight."

"Yes. Tell him it is."

Lung whispered, "God damn, I have hunger."

"The shinfoo asks, 'Where you come from, where you go?'"

"Tell him we come from Allied Headquarters in Chung-king."

Lung said, "Tell him we want goddam food."

"The shinfoo says what your and Lung's religion. I say it is apostles. He says being apostles is good. He will help study religion. We can stay here." He stopped. "I go to mass every day."

Lung spoke excitedly to Father Tan. A moment later Father Tan poured us wine and carefully put the cups in our hands.

WU'S A
COMMUNIST

GENERAL TONG and his guerrillas lived a few hundred yards from Hotien in a farmhouse that stood on the slope of a mountain. I had met the general when I arrived in Hotien and, with him, had attended frequent parties given by the town's leading citizens to honor China and America. The general was impatient. Headquarters feared enemy retaliation on civilians if he should attack the Japanese, and generals, of course, do not like headquarters telling them what to do. In the evenings when he came to visit us at the mission, General Tong explained sorrowfully his inability to fight the Japanese. His ammunition supply was so low that he had to account for each bullet fired by his troops—there were many things to give him headaches. But parties relieved the mind

of its problems, and when one became forgetfully drunk there
was no reason to be unhappy. We used to get drunk five or six
evenings a week. It was at a party given by General Tong that
I met General Wu.

"Tonight," Shum said one morning after breakfast, reading the invitation, a red, streamer-like piece of linen, "we have
party at best tea shop. General Tong gives party for honor
of General Wu, who is wounded in many places at Battle of
Shanghai and now lives in Hotien. He does not go out much,
for fear of ruining further his achievement. He's a Communist."

"Who's a Communist?" I asked slightly bewildered.

"Wu's a Communist," Shum said. "You have wounds?" he
added hopefully.

I said I had no wounds.

"You should have wound," he said.

In the evening Shum and I went to the best tea shop.
Shum led the way upstairs to a small front room partitioned
from the rooms in the back of the shop by a hedge of warped
wooden slats rising almost to the ceiling.

The table was round, the stools were round, and so was
General Wu. He was the roundest person I had ever seen,
and he proudly defeated my preconception that all Communists, even the Chinese members, must be lean and have a
hungry look in their eyes. His belly bounced when we shook
hands, and I would not have been surprised to see him rise in
the air like a Mardi Gras balloon. When I looked at his black
eyes, shining without depth, I felt he knew just what I was
thinking. Despite his preposterous girth and political inclina-
tion, Wu seemed to be more than a contemporary hero enjoying the homage of a brave defeat.

General Tong, maneuvering like a referee giving final instructions to boxers, thumped our backs enthusiastically, signaling the end of our sizing-up period. He gobbled to us in Chinese for a minute or two, then pointed a sharp finger at Shum, instructing him to tell me what was up.

"General Tong says wine make many friends," Shum said gingerly, as though his mind might be reaching for mnemonic references to the general's conversation. "War makes many friends, and some friends make enemies. But not always. General says he is not glad to have war, but glad that war gives you and General Wu chance to meet." Shum paused, lines of confusion creasing across his forehead, then continued in a lower, personal tone. "General Tong says General Wu is fierce lion and Communist, though he looks like new baby. General Tong does not desire Communists, but he says General Wu is only Communist in Hotien and can do nothing, and we have nothing to fear. General Tong says to never mind that General Wu's a Communist."

General Wu and I shook hands again.

Then we sat down at a round table dotted with blue archipelagoes of crockery, round islands of soups and rice and green vegetables. "President Roosevelt!" was toasted first, followed by "Chiang Kai-shek!" who was toasted five or six times before we got to "Churchill!" and "Stalin!" After proposing about eight toasts, I suddenly couldn't remember political and ideological leaders and I began toasting the girl tea shops in the town of Ho-Po and the Washington Senators. Before an hour had passed, we were all very drunk and had not eaten any food. Without warning, General Wu jumped up on the table and unbuttoned his shirt, placing his little finger on three wounds, dirt-purple scars on his chest and tubular arms.

Flinging his arms around and about, General Wu made a speech.

"General Wu says there are some Japs near here," Shum said. "They have no training for long time, and a few of them are going to forage tomorrow near San-Tien." The general stood firmly on the table, his arms akimbo. "He says we can surprise them. He wants to kill Japs. Do you?"

I looked at the general and nodded.

General Tong, who had followed the conversation with his eyes, like a spectator at a tennis match with cross-court volleys, smiled and yawned. He suggested that it was time to get some rest if we were going to fight in the morning. General Wu jumped resoundingly to the floor, and we toasted our operation against the Japanese, invoking the aid of numerous Chinese gods, hand grenades, and propitious clouds. We stumbled out of the best tea shop.

In the morning I was awakened in my bed on the mission's balcony by General Tong. Gray ground fogs lay settled like giant waffles in the valley. I had a hangover and didn't much care to get out of bed to fight some poor soldiers who were going foraging, but I climbed out, feeling sick in my stomach, and slowly dressed.

After a communal breakfast of rice and string beans, we left the mission and took to paddy paths that skirted Hotien. General Tong's guerrillas had assembled beyond the sentry tower before dawn to keep their movement secret from any spies in town. We found the guerrillas a few *li* (a *li* is about half a kilometer) out of Hotien; many were sleeping on the damp earth. The air was still and cool, and the sharp echoes of birds accompanied the roaring of the distant rapids. We waited quietly for a moment before we woke the guerrillas by singing the Chinese Nationalist "Marching Song," the opening words of which are "Arise, Arise, Go forward, Go forward." Gradually they shuffled barefooted into a line resembling a conga formed by sleepy dancers. We started walking. General Wu walked near Shum and me; the general wished that he had an American instrument of war, a pistol; he said he felt as though he were going to a fancy dress ball. We looked more like a troop out of Gilbert and Sullivan than a guerrilla band. I didn't know the quantity of our armament, and, except for two .45s and two carbines that Shum and I shared, I had fierce doubts of its quality. The guerrillas were tired; some were not too far from textbook examples of malnutrition. They took turns carrying about twelve heavy rifles of Balkan manufacture and four cartridge belts, and every man had his cumbersome wooden Czechoslovakian hand grenade, an awkward weapon in disguise. General Tong wore a .38 in a holster on his hip. We didn't see General Wu's pistol.

The pathway bordered the Nei-ho, where it ran through high brown hills with straggling patches of green and jack pines punched thinly on the hillsides. Soon we had to begin climbing and the river was perhaps three hundred feet below us. The earth was orange and wet, and with the first unshadowing of the sun it glistened like the back of a sleeping water buffalo. Slips of rock and mud forced us to walk singly. It was very steep, and the river became only a sound and strips of water crashing through the rocks. After two hours we stopped climbing and walked down the path carefully to a wider one beside the river. At a little trading town the river cut nobly into a barricade of low hills and marched on down through the green concatenations to the ocean. After a short distance we left the river and walked fast toward a mountain range rising southward. By eleven o'clock we were on top of a very flat mountain that was a couple of horizons higher than the mountain chains on either side. At a tea stall we stopped and had a meal of tea and rice, and as soon as we finished eating we moved on. Trees and shadows from clouds tufted themselves in unpatterned groups: trees as tall as the wind, shadows of clouds, and clouds of shadows. The land was like countryside plowed in crazy furrows, hyphenated by shadows of inland-flying gulls, blue and white streaks, jetting above without curiosity.

San-Tien lay in a cove to our right, between a mountain and a hill. The mountain declined sharply and touched a green river valley, with a sun-silver line of a stream reflecting through it like a dagger, spreading from the cove. We looked down in the valley and followed the line of vision in a slow panorama.

"General Tong says Japs will be down there in thirty minutes," Shum said as he unslung his carbine. "Thinks it is best for us to go down and get across to other side and hide. He say we may kill many Japs before they see us."

Thick oases of bamboos clustered in the valley on the other side of the stream. We descended the mountain on a rocky path and came to the drift in the land where the slope began to be terraced into rice paddies; then we were in the valley. We crossed narrow paddy paths, moving swiftly to the banks of the stream, which, because of its speed, seemed strangely foreign in the slow, hot air. Walking upstream we came to a foot-plank bridge. One plank was warped more than the others, and Shum nearly lost his balance crossing it. Before we got across the bridge we heard a shot.

We got to the slope of the mountain beyond San-Tien

in less than an hour, from which point we looked down over the area we had just traversed. There had been no more rifle shots. General Tong covered the valley stream with his field glasses. "General Tong say look there," Shum said, pointing toward the stream and farther up from the bridge.

Tong handed me the glasses, and in a matter of seconds I focused them on this scene: a number of green-and-brown-clad figures gathered together in the silent and rough green foliage.

"General Tong says let us charge softly. They are Japs."

Shum said he was going to act as a communicator and guide; hands motioned other hands to proceed quietly to the periphery of the bamboos. With the exception of the stream side, we had the foragers surrounded. Those of us facing the water potted a few clips into the bamboos. Then we moved closer. I saw two Japanese uniforms, aimed my carbine at one, and fired four rounds. They were no more than fifty feet from me, but evidently I had been a poor shot.

Shum came over, grimacing. "Don't shoot any more," he said. "General Wu's in there and Japs have escaped. We shoot only at uniforms. The general says they take off uniforms and stand them up in mysterious ways to make us think they are in there. They are not. They get in river and swim away; all but one." We moved in the thicket and counted fifteen uniforms. "General Wu says he is damned," Shum said. He pointed to the general standing over one dead Japanese, half-dressed and wearing a pistol.

General Tong and Shum whispered to each other, and then Shum told me to come with them deeper into the bamboos. The guerrillas were dividing the Japanese uniforms.

"General Tong found that General Wu has no pistol. He says it is nice if we give Jap pistol to General Wu," Shum said.

"That's fine," I said.

We went back to General Wu. General Tong stooped and picked up the pistol from the dead soldier and gave it to General Wu, who accepted the trophy and bowed as low as his girth permitted. Wasting no time, for it was early afternoon and we had to return to Hotien that day, the guerrillas began to dress in articles of clothing that the fifteen intelligent Japanese had left behind.

I asked General Tong if we wouldn't scare somebody on our return. No, I was told, and in order not to scare anybody we would sing the "Marching Song" as loud as we could whenever we met anyone. So we started back, General Tong, General Wu, and I, walking arm in arm when the terrain was agreeable and singing at the tops of our lungs, although it was not necessary.

It was past midnight when we reached Hotien. The guerrillas dropped wearily in the doorways of the small shops, but we four went on to the mission house and started drinking again in my radio room off the balcony. In the early morning, as chilling winds began blowing in from the garden, we went outside, past the servants' quarters, to a plot of wet grass. A few tulips nodded their sleepy heads at two ducks waddling by. The priest's black mongrel, Do-Do, lying sphinxlike, opened one eye, looked at the ducks, then at us, and closed his eye. Our battle was over but he wasn't interested.

"There are names for battle actions?" Shum asked.

"Yes," I said.

"General Wu says will you please name our fight."

I thought a few minutes. "I know," I said. "We'll call it Operation Cooperation."

Shum smiled and talked to General Wu. As soon as Shum finished, the general shook our hands, excused himself, and left for his house in Hotien. General Tong sighed, then he spoke gruffly.

"The general says war is crazy," Shum said, watching the figure of General Wu jogging into Hotien.

HEROES TREATED
LIKE NOT HEROES

NOT MANY days after our victory over the Japanese for-agers, a message came from headquarters ordering Shum and Lung and me to return to Hingning with all equipment. The message gave no reason, and even when we arrived at head-quarters, we weren't told what was up. Major Fletcher sent for me as soon as we arrived. He was seated at his desk. "I'll be damned, Pinck, if I see how you did what you did," he said in such a bewildered tone that he seemed to imply that I knew what he was talking about. I didn't know, and I told him so.

"You don't know, Pinck," he said incredulously.

"Nosir."

"I'll be damned."

"Yessir."

"You *realize* what you did?" He didn't believe that I honestly didn't know.

"I don't," I said.

"You don't." He combed his hands through his thinning gray hair. "God." He picked up a green pencil and accomplished a variety of modernistic doodles. Then he nodded his head sadly and said, "After all I told you . . ."

I nodded the way he nodded, sideways (incredulity) and up and down (flabbergastedness). Fletcher was alternately a devil cursing himself and a preacher imploring God on a dry-run sermon. These hagiolatries got on my nerves, and I thought how good it would feel to tell the major that I, too, knew His name. But I kept quiet, and shortly he calmed down and said in a voice loaded with repugnance and confusion, "I don't get it, Pinck." And, after pausing and looking directly at the door, he said, "I'll let you know as soon as I do." So I left the office knowing nothing except that I was in a definite mess and I should have known what it was.

Shum and Lung were called in to see Fletcher, and when, after a few minutes, they came out of his office, they told me they would have to live in a Hingning hotel. They had to leave immediately and were forbidden to see me at any time. They stuck out their hands for me to shake as though they were pallbearers about to lift a casket. "See you!" said Shum.

"I think never mind," said Lung, puckering his lower lip into a philosophic half-moon. And then they picked up their two suitcases and left.

Headquarters consisted of four one-story buildings that had previously been part of a middle school on the outskirts of Hingning. Low, close to one another, and alabaster white on the walls both inside and out, one building was an office that housed maps and safes and white-gowned Chinese who were advisers or servants, or both, and another structure, a thatched-roof Gauguinesque bungalow with a few bamboos at each corner, like soldiers at attention, was Fletcher's house, and he was its only occupant. There was the dining room, with its screen door so narrow that even the Chinese cooks had to go through it sideways. The phlegmatic American technicians slept in the longest building; lines of rope beds with boxes of mosquito netting above them gave this room the appearance of a small hangar. I threw my bags in an empty corner of the room and claimed an empty bed. The first few days I got up early enough to have breakfast with the major and the other men, for I felt, no matter what the trouble I was in, that this would create a favorable impression and possibly elicit some sympathy from the major. After breakfasting four days in a row and receiving bothersome, longnosed glances from Fletcher, I said to hell with it and stopped getting up so early. At lunch and supper I was the recipient of his quiet composure. That was enough. The technicians seemed to have a desire to become educated, or maybe they just wanted to find out what I knew. In the morning, at noon rest, in the evening, they asked questions, and they repeated themselves daily in a litany devoted to sex, food, and electricity. Between the meals and the major and the inquisitive Americans, I was having a hard time.

One evening after I had been a week at headquarters, another American, who had driven down from Chihkiang, where there was a secret airfield, came into our building. He surveyed the room and me and then dragged his belongings to my corner. "Howdy, buddy," he said. He threw his bag on the next bed, sat down, then turned his head to the side and stared at me from the corners of his eyes, which were magnified by thick lenses of Army-issued spectacles. He looked like a blond Mongolian, with cheek bones so sharp and wide and high that they appeared a functional part of his nose. Then he smiled and I thought of a Halloween pumpkin.

He pressed his hands down on the ropes. "Damn bed damn uncomfortable," he said. "No give. Naw hell."

"Rough," I said.

"Mind if I sack it here?"

I told him surely not, go ahead.

He said thanks and arranged his stuff on the floor. Then he lay down and began asking questions. Questions, more esoteric than those of the other men, that made me feel uncomfortably like a contestant on a quiz program. Did I like my girl? What was it like out in the field, did I get scared? Didn't I think Sherman was correct in his summation of war —it wasn't fun, was it? He told me his name was Albert Wells Pettijohn and he hated the Albert and the Pettijohn—he wanted to be called Wells. After an hour I told Wells to shut up. "Okay," he said, and went to sleep.

Clouds scudded low and gray the next morning, and the dampness in the air made it uncomfortable to stay in bed. I got up and went to the dining room. Major Fletcher was seated alone, staring dispiritedly at his rice bowl.

He asked how I liked breakfast. Fine, I told him.

"God," he said flatly. "God damn."

That did not require an answer. I felt that I would rather submit to a sermonful of "God" and "God damn" than another question from the technicians.

"God, Pinck."

I paid no attention.

"I'll be a pisscomplected well digger." There was no emotion in his voice. "You still don't have any idea what's wrong?"

"Nosir."

"God."

Suddenly he became loud. "How the hell could you disobey my orders so flagrantly?"

"I didn't disobey your orders," I said. "What orders?"

"It's this, Pinck," he said, leveling a fork at my nose. "You went off on a military expedition against the Nips. You killed one goddam Nip. Hell! We could bomb Hirohito's palace this minute, but it wouldn't be strategic. I hope you know what that means. If we bombed the little fellow the Nips would send kamikaze planes—hell, *armies* to the West Coast. And I've got my family in California."

He put down his fork. "Why did you go off on the expedition?" he said. "I want to know why."

Expedition, hell, I thought, it was more like a Cub Scout field trip. "I more or less had to," I said, hoping that I would soon have an opportunity to change the conversational ground. "I attended a party for General Wu who's a—" Some grace rescued me from saying Communist; I gulped, cleared my throat, and continued: "—hero of the Battle of Shanghai. He showed us his wounds and wanted to know if I had any wounds to show. He was disappointed when he found out that I had none and suggested that we attack a few hungry Japs who were going to forage the next day near San-Tien. He knew it would be a small detachment and said we might pretend that we were meeting them accidentally."

"God."

"I said this might not be the thing to do and gave your reasons. I said the Japs would retaliate by killing women and children, and General Tong, who was giving the party, said they'd been doing that all the time. I couldn't back out. But I wasn't keen for it. There was hardly any warfare, and when I left Hotien after your message, there hadn't been any report of retaliation. General Tong says there won't be any."

"General Tong!" the major roared as though the name were an epithet. "He's in Hingning, too. You didn't know that, did you?"

"Nosir."

"He is, and he's getting plenty of hell."

"He's a general," I said.

"There are enough Chinese generals around here to form an army. They'll take care of him."

"What are you going to do with me?" I asked timidly.

"I could court-martial you. Send you to the salt mines, you know."

He smiled, so I tried to smile respectfully.

He laughed aloud. "By God, I could break you," he said.

"You certainly could, you could break me all to hell," I said enthusiastically.

Then he looked at me cautiously. "I really don't get it," he said. "If Albert says you're okay, well all right. We'll—" Major Fletcher stopped talking. We noticed Albert Wells Pettijohn standing inside the gauze-screen door.

"Come on in, Albert," the major said. "The rice is fine, Albert."

Albert Wells Pettijohn winced. The major said to him, "You heard what I've been talking about?"

"You bet."

Fletcher stood up. "Albert is a doctor. I sent for him to find out if you're all there." The major walked quickly to the door.

"Call me by my middle name, please—it's Wells," Albert Wells Pettijohn said.

"Wells," I said.

"Now that you know my business there's no use beating around the bush. Nobody's crazy in your family?" he asked.

"No," I answered.

"I mean relatives," he explained.

"No."

"You really don't think you did a bad thing, I mean in reference to why Major Fletcher sent for me?"

I shrugged my shoulders. "I see my error," I said, "but I don't really feel that I'll cause a revolution."

"Hell, I don't either," said Wells. "Wish I had a chance to fight some Japs."

"Wasn't much of a fight."

"The major said it would be up to me to decide if you're all right or not. As far as I'm concerned, you're all right."

"I'm glad of that."

The doctor furrowed his rice, then looked up suddenly and asked sharply, "You know how I learned the facts of life?"

"No," I said.

"My father asked me if I knew how to make a woman pregnant. I told him I did. Well, he told me, it was just the same with the birds and the bees."

I laughed.

"Hell, yes, you're okay," he said. "Either you have it or you don't. That's something the major doesn't understand. He doesn't have it."

I didn't know what he was talking about, but I said I thought so, too.

A slow-moving genial-eyed woman, with her hands behind her, came to the table and asked us if we wanted more rice; the moment we said yes, she brought her arms around, holding two bowls of rice. She placed them before us and silently glided away to the kitchen. At the door she turned around for a look and smiled. I smiled at her, but Wells grumpily chomped his rice. He was concentrating.

"I think I'd better ask you some more questions," he said cautiously. "They're questions that are always asked, you know?"

"All right," I said.

"So, if it's all right with you, well, I'll start asking them."

"Okay," I said.

"You like movies?" he asked.

"Yes."

"What kind best?"

"Good ones best," I replied.

"Westerns?"

"Not usually."

"What's the last movie you saw before coming out here?"

"*Saratoga Trunk.*"

"You like it?"

"Yes," I said. "I liked it very much."

"Who was in it?" he asked.

"Ingrid Bergman."

"You like her?"

"Very much."

"Was there a male in the cast?"

"Yes," I replied. "Gary Cooper."

"Did you like him?"

"Yes."

"Who did you like best, Bergman or Cooper?"

"Bergman."

"Would you like her with you now?"

"Yeah, man," I said.

"Did you ever have a nervous breakdown?" he asked.

"No," I said.

"Do you like the Army?"

"Of course not," I said.

"You like to make the Army your career?"

"Are you crazy?"

"Would you like to live in China?"

"Good God," I said.

"You like girls?" he asked.

"Jesus Christ," I said.

"You like the Chinese?" he asked finally, with a haunted look.

"Yes," I said. "I like them."

"I don't!" he said furiously. "I don't! They're after me." He swallowed a mouthful of rice. "They got a knife in my back a foot long."

"Yes," I said.

"Wait till you've been out here as long as I have," he said. "They'll knife you, too." He made a noise with his tongue, intending to sound like a dull knife rending flesh.

"Goddam," I said.

In the afternoon the major called me to his office; he said the doctor believed I was sane and that, as far as he was concerned, I was sane but he still didn't get it. He said I could go back to Hotien; I thanked him and left the office. My first stop was the hotel in Hingning.

Shum and Lung were drinking tea in their room at the hotel when I arrived. I told them what had happened.

"Good, good," said Shum, shaking my hand. "That makes me pleasure."

Lung did not get up. Raising one eyebrow to an arch of discernment, he said simply, "Now we go to Hotien."

"What's happened to General Tong?" I asked.

"Good," Shum said.

"Good what?"

"Chinese headquarters have General Tong in Hingning."

"I know that," I said impatiently. "I mean what are they going to do with him?"

"Lung hears from Chinese headquarters that they wait to see what happens to you before it happens to General Tong. That means the general goes back to Hotien. That is good," Shum said.

Lung proposed a toast to our success. He threw the tea on the floor and filled the pot with wine. Then he poured wine into three cups.

"They thought you are crazy," Shum said carefully, not looking at me. Lung laughed, then swallowed his wine in one gulp.

"They no longer think that," I said.

"Good," Shum said.

"Damn good," Lung said.

Shum said he would make arrangements for the general to meet us at the Sui Chi River the following morning. We drank the bottle of wine, then Shum and Lung went to the Chinese headquarter's compound and I went back to the American compound.

At an unreasonably early hour in the morning, we were driven to the river. We hired a sampan that was tied in the shade of bamboos, arranged our baggage on the boat, and waited in the shade for General Tong. After an hour of growing morning heat, he appeared in a rickshaw on the rise of the road. Shum and I ran to meet him.

General Tong had lost his pep—he did not pump my hand. Though I was happy and glad to see him, I shook his hand in the same sad manner. Had there been any hair on his head before his ordeal at headquarters, it would probably have turned white. As it was, new lines had come to his scalp, worry lines that ought to be only on a man's forehead.

"The general says war is woe," Shum said. "Must have no more war with Japs, he is ordered by Chinese headquarters. We must not bother Japs."

I bowed my head.

"The general says he is sad to think of heroes being treated like not heroes."

Shum put his hand on General Tong's shoulders, and we turned down the road. In a few minutes we reached the bamboo shade, jumped aboard the sampan, and began moving with the current in sunny midstream of the Sui Chi River.

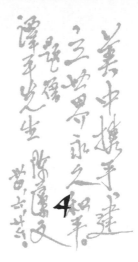

HA IS A
MAD HARRY

SEVERAL AFTERNOONS later, as we were taking show-
ers from buckets on the balcony of the mission house, Lung
came up to me and said, "Ai-yah."

That was all he said. Then he sighed ponderously.

"Silly bastard," came Shum's voice from the other end of
the balcony.

Shum walked across the balcony toward us and snapped
his towel at Lung's hand. "Silly bastard has girl friend," he said.

"You're married, Lung," I said. His wife was more than
160 kilos away, in a town west of Canton.

"This girl in Hotien, just girl friend," Lung explained.

"All right," I said. "What's all the bother about?"

"I like to visit her tonight. You know?"

"Know what?"

Lung turned to Shum. "How to say?" he asked Shum. "You say, please."

"He means he wants to spend night with her," Shum said. "Lung wants to have girl for wife in Hotien. Chinese marriage, he says."

I said that it wouldn't be safe: there were, after all Japanese soldiers not too far from us, and if we should have to evacuate Hotien in a hurry at night, it wouldn't help us to have our radio operator sleeping in a hard-to-find mudhole of a house.

Shum spoke to Lung. When he finished, Lung pushed him aside. "Plenty safe," Lung said. "Better than go to girls in Ho-Po."

"He say he stay with her before," said Shum. "When we first come here, he sleep all night with her. Come back, though, in time for schedule."

"Never late," said Lung. "Damn nice girl."

"Does she know you're married?" I asked him.

"Marriage no difference," he said. "I not hear from wife for long time. Only when she wants money. No letters, only asks for money. This girl in Hotien asks for me. No money." Lung blinked his eyes a few times, and a new thought seemed to be taking shape in his mind. "You want girl?" he said quickly.

"Never mind," I said. "Bastard."

"No, Mister Dan, not bastard," he said emphatically. "I know bastard. Not bastard. I love this girl. You know?"

"I love you so much, you tell me how much," said Shum.

"No. Real love. Not fooling."

Lung was at the halfway point, not knowing whether we were joking or being serious.

"My girl nice," said Lung, smiling piously. "She very poor. Almost prostitute." Then he looked meekly at me.

"Silly bastard, silly bastard!" Shum howled. "He means *destitute.*"

"Where you learn how to speaking English?" I asked them.

Neither said anything for a few moments.

"I know," Shum said suddenly. "Lung can marry her. Chinese marriage."

Shum said it would be all right for Lung to have his woman with him in the mission house providing he married her. He spoke in a hypercritical *I*-don't-want-a-woman tone.

"I'm married," Lung said abruptly, and then paused. "All right for me to do," he continued softly. "In movies Americans get many wives for sleeping."

I told him, patly, that we were in a war.

"No wives for sleeping in war?" he asked.

So with Shum's advice I gave Lung permission to marry his woman and have her live with him in his first floor room, which faced the front courtyard. Lung laughed and ran out of the mission compound and into Hotien. In less than an hour he returned, holding by the hand a girl whose loveliness was centered at first glance in her lynx-colored eyes. She wore a black silk suit, trousers, and a blouse with buttons running diagonally down from her breast to her hip; pigtails, caught by two rubber bands holding vases of black hair, came down in front to the level of the highest button. "This is Ha," Lung said. "She loves me."

Shum sat down on a bench and stared at her.

"Now you meet," Lung continued evenly, "now Ha and I go sleeping." And the two of them went downstairs.

During the days that followed, Lung became happier and happier while Shum and I found our tempers growing shorter and shorter. Then one day something happened that put an end to our short tempers. One night Shum nudged me from sleep and said, in a whisper, "Be quiet. I think Ha is Mad Harry."

"Mad what?" I asked.

"Mad Harry," Shum repeated, putting a finger on his lips as a signal to shhhh. "Ha is Mad Harry!"

"You're a Mad Shum," I said. "What the hell's wrong with you?"

"Do not make noise," he warned, making another lips-and-finger signal.

"No noise," I repeated.

"For best safety, you better know now I think Ha is Mad Harry."

"Ha is Ha."

"Do not joke," said Shum.

"All right. First you tell me what is a Mad Harry."

"Mad Harry," Shum explained, "was famous German spy in first World War. Woman. Name was Mad Harry. Ha is Mad Harry. I have feeling. Do not make noise, and I will tell you my plan to trap Mad Harry." He told me his plan: he would tell Lung with Ha within hearing distance that our area would soon see four hundred real soldiers who were going to fight against the Japanese in a two-day guerrilla battle that would shelve the Japanese in Southeast China for the rest of the war. Fifty of the soldiers would be American, the rest would be stout-hearted Chinese. He would advise Lung to keep this information secret.

The plan seemed pretty good to me. In a war that wasn't fought in your own language it was difficult to determine what was according to Lao-tze, the Hoyle of China, and what was not.

"I will take care of it," said Shum grimly, walking softly back to his bed at the other end of the balcony. "I give my word."

Two weeks went by, and then, in the third week, as I was watching Lung receive messages from headquarters, Shum burst in upon me with the news that he had the proof to show that Ha was a real Mad Harry.

"Her heart is black," he said.

"How black?" I asked.

"Black as an ace," he answered. "Ha is real Mad Harry. Today one of our agents hear Japs in Swatow talking, say four thousand husky Americans and many times that number Chinese come to kill them." Shum looked at Lung. "That is proof Ha is Mad Harry."

I suggested that Lung might have told it to someone in Hotien who in turn had given it to the Japanese. At any rate, we ought to question him. Perhaps our radio operator might have an inkling of the nature of his wife's other work; thinking of Ha, who was still in bed, it was understandable why Lung would want to keep such inconveniencing information private. Shum agreed; we would quiz Lung.

The moment Lung took off his earphones, we went at him; Shum in Chinese, I in English. Lung, dazed and dit-dit-dah-happy, tried to answer in both languages and failed to make himself understood in either. A pulse began throbbing against the sweaty skin of his forehead, and another on his cheek, beneath his sideburn. To turn from the dits and dahs of the hot-fingered radio operator at headquarters to the confluence of low English and high Chinese was indeed capable of wilting the energy and mental process of any man, much less Lung, whose native language was really Morse code. Lung clumped exhaustedly on the table, his head resting beside the radio.

Shum put his hand on Lung's shoulder and spoke to him quietly. Lung raised his head to a forty-five-degree angle; his hand was palm-flat over his ear. "What go on here?" he asked.

"Number three degree," I said.

"Do not like number three degree."

"We only want to ask you some questions, Lung. We don't mean to pounce on you."

"Do not know *pounce*," Shum said expectantly. I told him that this wasn't the time to learn English.

Shum and Lung lapsed into a rather mellifluous Chinese. When they finished talking to each other, Shum said, "Lung say Ha is not spy he knows, but cannot say for sure. Nothing is sure, he says. Lung says how can Ha tell Japs, he never lets Ha out of sight, sleeps all night together, talks all day together, no time to tell Japs. Lung says he tells nobody but Ha about the guerrillas. He says he hates Japs, would slit her throat and other places if she is spy. Lung says it is unusual how Japs know real soldiers come."

"Ask Lung if he'll help us get proof that Ha is Mad Harry," I said.

When Shum and Lung finished speaking, Shum said,

"Lung says he would not care to sleep with Ha if she is spy. Would not care to give her so much fun. He asks can he still sleep with Ha to get proof?"

I nodded yes. Lung got up and quickly left the radio room.

"Ha's days are numbers," said Shum with messianic fierceness.

It all seemed a big joke to me; in the days that followed I would tell Lung different kinds of unusual information. "Sixty-seven armored tugboats are going to land next Wednesday at two o'clock at Lukfeng." Or "Six hundred B-17s are going to drop ten thousand bombs on Nip headquarters in Swatow Bay." I hoped to hear from my agents how the Japanese would paraphrase such intelligence, but the Japanese in the tea shops in Swatow and in towns farther south never mentioned this news within earshot of our agents. The Japanese stuck to the original information about the soldiers; in a tea shop in Lukfeng the number of real soldiers had increased to five thousand and, notwithstanding the reputed sobriety of the Japanese commander in Haifeng, named Tin Boon, rank of colonel, my best agent in that town, a twelve-year-old boy, reported hearing Tin Boon swear, by the seven suns that ripen apples on the island of Hokkaido, that seven thousand hard-backed Americans and one hundred armed Chinese were planning a long and furious pitched battle that would rage from Swatow to Waichow.

If our own intelligence had not become so paltry, I suppose I would have taken more serious notice of Ha and helped Shum to find ways of obtaining proof of her guilt. Our messages to headquarters contained no more valuable information than, for instance, this military masquerade: "In Swabue inside warehouse on Yi Ma Road are five hundred straw-grass soldiers, dressed in yellow uniforms and armed with wooden guns." Swabue was a port town, the first of naval usage above Hong Kong. Maybe the straw-grass soldiers were a secret weapon; maybe they had been sewn together in order to represent a large force to the husky, attacking Americans; perhaps they were really Japanese and not straw-grass soldiers.

Ha came one morning into the dank, recently white-washed radio room. I was scraping lime off a few articles that had been put on the table too soon after the painting: a couple of books, an empty holster. One book, the Boy Scouts' handbook, I had taken overseas upon the advice of a retired public health official. I had noticed on several occasions that my handbook had been moved. After a while I had to go to the W.C., and when I got back, I found Ha standing in the corner near the window with the book in her hands.

"Ha!" I said. "How are you, you lovely bitch? What the hell are you doing with my Boy Scout handbook?"

She had moved quickly to put the book back on the table when I first came in, but when she detected the friendly note in my voice, she winked and turned back to the book.

"Ha, how'd you manage to get away from Lung, you old Mad Harry?"

Ha recognized the name of her husband. With her hands rubbing on her face, she told me that Lung was washing himself. She came to the table and put her hand on the radio and leafed through the pages of the handbook, smiling and winking at me. She discovered a page she wanted explained. It was a two-page spread, a map drawn in fine scale, showing topographical heights, displacements, latrines, roads, trees, paths, water towers, an airfield runway, and a small farmhouse.

There was a key to the map, and its title, in very small letters in the bottom corner of the left page, was "Getting to Mrs. Nestor's Farm."

Ha placed a finger on the map and then opened her palm upward, signifying utter lack of knowledge. She put the book in my hands, her finger pressed on the map. I lifted up her finger and found that it covered a latrine surrounded by trees. With my hands I swooped the air with loops and half-successful Immelmanns. "Airplanes, Ha! Kill little cucumber bastards!" Then I made a tommy gun. "Cuts off Jap legs one inch above the knee, Ha!" This, I told her, was what the map meant, and I indicated that it was a big secret by putting my finger to my lips. Ha seemed to understand. She nodded and put her finger to her lips. She leafed through the pages of the book again and left the room.

That evening at supper there was no Ha. Lung said she had not returned from the W.C. where she had gone shortly before suppertime. Maybe she had fallen in, Shum suggested to me and, in Chinese, to Lung. Lung frowned and looked worried. We began eating our rice and had already finished one bowl and were working on the second when Shum got up from the table and said, "Ha is flew!"

We ran downstairs, got three bodyguards (who were sitting in the front courtyard juggling their hand grenades), and headed into town. The streets were fairly crowded and Shum found many people to direct us. He would speak to a bystander or a merchant in front of his store who immediately would lift his hand and swing it in a direction. I asked Shum what he was asking these men. His translation, in brisk English, was, "Where did that rotten, beautiful girl who sleeps with Lung go?" Everyone, it seemed, was able to give a direction.

There was soon not much left of Hotien in which to look. Finally, we turned into the best tea shop and, guided by the frightened owner, ran upstairs to a private room in the back. In a corner on the floor sat Ha, glaring at us. Shum spoke excitedly to the owner. "He says she come and ask to spend night here. Probably to leave Hotien in the morning, when light strikes the earth." Lung and Ha immediately launched into a heavy conversation; dark words flew about. The sullen, lovely girl on a musty straw mat stared resentfully at us for a moment then suddenly attempted an aviatorial stunt that met with instant failure. Lung pushed her back heavily to the floor and pulled off her trousers. In that place from which all of us enter the world, Lung found a roll of papers, the shape and texture of which reminded me of code messages. He gave them to Shum, who began reading them. The papers contained information about the three of us and information we had sent to headquarters. Then I noticed in Shum's hands something familiar: two pages from the Boy Scouts' handbook—the map called "Getting to Mrs. Nestor's Farm."

"Ha, you are dirty, unsanitary spy," Shum exploded.

Ha, standing beautifully naked in the corner of the darkened room, told him, in flawless sign language, to perform a biological impossibility.

YOU YELLING ME, YACKSON

IN THE center of the courtyard of the mission there was a shallow tile pool. The water rose about a foot and barely lapped at the flat, narrow edge. In the morning the sunlight nailed its rays on the pool and on the surrounding walls bearing the posters of the generalissimo. Sometime after dinner the sunlight began angling away from the pool and up the walls, and by five in the evening the courtyard was shaded and cool, and occasionally breezes that seemed to have come straight down pushed the water in gentle, straight-lined rows. If the shinfoo had bothered himself to visit the courtyard in the late afternoon he would have seen an English class in session, the members of the class sitting around the pool listening to me lecturing on the most valuable English expressions, ones that would most benefit them in any discourse with any English-speaking person they might someday meet. This the shinfoo never bothered to do; he said he always had an important engagement with a member of his flock before suppertime and couldn't, even for the sake of friendship between China and America, get away. For the laymen who attended the classes, mostly a few refugees from professional positions in Canton and a serious group of local civilians, there was no harm in learning my English.

When I started the course, at the humble insistence of our poker-playing friend, a former Canton detective, Charley Lau, I had intended to teach them proper English. I envisioned the Chinese walking through Hotien of an evening, greeting one another with "Hello" and "How are you?" I got into trouble during the first session when Shum, who was proudly showing his skill as an interpreter to our friends, decided his English was better than mine.

"You speak bad English," he said during the class, in an aside to me. "You say too much cussing."

"The hell with you," I replied, aware of a feeling of spectator tension in the courtyard. "I don't need you around here. Charley Lau knows French and he can be my interpreter. I'll tell him the words and sounds. He can tell them just as well as you."

"You speak bad English," Shum repeated, walking away from the gathering.

Charley Lau had a chewing gum smile. He was a friendly man of perhaps thirty-five, rather sharp in appearance. He did not wear Chinese clothes but instead dressed in white, blue-striped flannel trousers and a white cotton shirt buttoned at the neck. He had a reputation as an important detective;

he had studied detective methods in Japan and France and, he told me, through Shum, in the "New York City metropolis" with many detectives. He produced a card to prove it. The card asked that the courtesy of the city be given its holder. The fact that Lau had spent some time in New York but didn't remember any English made me think he wasn't particularly smart. But he was friendly and genuinely seemed to believe in the unity of our two countries. I never beat him in a card game.

Once, during an unexpected setback in a poker game, Lau, quite distinctly, said, "Sacré merde!"

"You old bastard!" I said, and asked him in French if he spoke French, a language I had taken in college. He said he did, and after the game we talked about his detective success. He wouldn't admit to English, even when I tried to get him excited during the next hand. Lau still clicked his tongue, grinned, and burst out with the same expression.

So Charley Lau took over the interpretation for the class. He and I would converse in front of the group in French. I would tell him what the expression that I was going to say in English meant, and he would memorize the English without knowing the individual words.

The class went on in French. And no one seemed to learn anything. What was taught in one class would have to be taught again. The students couldn't remember. This lack of aptitude got on my nerves. I wanted to end the English class, but Shum advised against it, for fear of making too many enemies.

Cantonese, of course, was spoken in our area. In general, I was told by Shum and Lau, the words of Cantonese ended in consonants. (Mandarin, spoken in most of China, ended in vowels.) Shum remembered old boards advertising the "Hang-on Company, Building Contractors," in Hong Kong. He thought English was the funniest language in the world.

His own English was consistently inconsistent and inconsistently consistent. Often words he had learned in medical school sprang forth during a conversation and startled me. His English was not basic; it ranged from the semi-illiterate to the technically skilled, varying only slightly in the large middle ground of words and grammar. Sometimes a word would be apostrophes and sometimes it wouldn't, although its use was the same and in the old position in the sentence. Shum's favorite English word was *bastard*, and he could say it very well.

"Bastard!" I would suddenly remark.

"Bastard!" Shum would answer with intellectual enthusiasm, expecting to be drilled in English.

The polylingual cursing that went on at the mission might have given evidence of an intelligent society, if the cursing were accompanied on occasion by serious conversation. It never was. For the most part, my conversation was concerned with the necessities of the day: getting up, eating, the weather, intelligence, Japs, going to bed. You didn't need to know too much of a language to find out something about those necessities. Bull sessions were tiresome. Shum had a hard time, and so did I. "Bastard!" took the place of many conversations.

During class I would say, "Eh bien, Charley Lau, allons. Est-ce que vous me dites, Jackson? C'est-à-dire . . ."

The class responded in a chorus. "You yelling me, Yackson!"

As the key word to bring on this response, I told them one must immediately say "You yelling me, Yackson" when they heard the word *hot*.

If I met one of the men in town, after supper, sometimes I would say to him, "It's goddam hot, Brother Sing." And Sing would smile proudly and reply, "You yelling me, Yackson."

I also taught the English class to sing "Dinah," which they liked more than any song they had heard in recent years. They liked singing it best at the end of the study period, when the cooks began carrying black pots of greens and rice to different rooms off the courtyard and when the shinfoo began his evensong services.

"Eh bien, Charley Lau, attendez merci. C'est-à-dire . . ."

For a favor done, the class learned to say, "Sanka you all, Yackson." And an inquiry into the state of one's health was, "How's your furf burner?"

They considered "key" words the epitome of their education in English and hoped for the day when another man who spoke English might chance to come to their village. "Imagine their surprise at meeting so many cultured men in the hills of Kwangtung, all speaking English. What a surprise for the traveler," was the way they transported their thoughts to me through Lau. "How impressive."

Since they liked to learn key words, I kept busy thinking up unusual responses. I hoped that they never met another man who spoke English while I was in town. If they did, the cooperation and good feeling would end and I might well be forced to leave town to escape a posse of the members of the class. And Charley Lau, even though he always took my money at poker, would probably be leading them.

I thought about my teaching English a lot and decided

that I liked it. Many stories about the men in China told how they had succumbed to their problems; some used alcohol and were shipped back to the States as alcoholics; some had trouble with their stomachs—ulcers and amoebic dysentery; and others lost their minds, that is, the Army considered them psychos. They had gone "China happy" or had lost their balance because the fear of the enemy had become too strong ever to forget at any time during the day or night, or they had been a little off before they were sent behind the lines. One way I thought I could beat that was to have a hell of a good time. Like teaching the Chinese to speak English. My English. What the hell.

On this day we were seated on the ledge around the pool. It was cool and pleasant, and Mr. Pan and Mr. Chong had taken off their sandals and were soaking their feet in water. The subject of the day was key words, the most emphatic words in expressions that Shum and I used a number of times daily, such as "hell" and "nuts" and "damn" and "goddam."

Every man seemed to be happy.

We were enjoying our lesson and had reached "Dinah"; pleading with her to stay where she was, we vowed to hop on the nearest ocean liner to follow her to where we were, when Shum entered the courtyard. He had a page of the code pad in his hand.

I nodded to him to join in the song.

He shook his head.

As soon as the song ended, Shum rushed over. "What the hell is this?" he shouted.

Led by Lau, who raised his hand like a conductor, the class said in unison, "Yes, it is a lovely day. "

Shum appeared stunned. He put his hand on his forehead.

"Par excellence, n'est-ce pas?" said Lau.

"I am damned!" Shum said.

Lau raised his hand to the class. "Yes, we are expecting rain to fall now," they chorused with enthusiasm.

"Dan, you're nuts!" Shum exploded.

"You health, I hope!" The members of the English class were excited. This was a totally unexpected opportunity to practice their English. They stood up and formed a circle around us.

Shum calmed himself and spoke to them, in Chinese. They bowed their heads dejectedly.

Then he whispered to me, "This is enough. I tell them important work has come up to take you away from teaching. Work about the war. I tell them you regret having to end the English class, but maybe they will have even better opportunity in the future." Shum stopped. He stared at the members of the class as they began leaving through the mission door. "I think you're . . . ," he said, throwing a ball of paper into the pool.

We three: radio operator Lung Chiu Wah (*left*) and interpreter Shum Hay. Our survival and success was primarily due to Shum's judgment and skill.

Col. Tin Boon, leader of the Japanese troops in my area. Although his rank is uncertain, he has too many decorations to be anything less than a colonel, I'm told. I had great animus toward him during the war, but my feeling was slightly tempered after the war, upon reflecting that he could so easily have ordered me captured or killed. Why he didn't, I'll never know.

The chief of staff of the Nationalist government's Seventh War Area, Lau Chi Man, occasionally visited us. He was modest, capable, and friendly and never doubted that Japan would be defeated.

This dinner invitation, printed on purple paper, was translated for me by Shum Hay. I recall that beetles, wine, and rice were featured every day at this restaurant. I never ate a cooked or uncooked beetle.

Japanese soldiers who operated near me in a game of hide-and-seek. They sought me and I hid from them. My agents along the coast brought me this photograph.

I received this certificate at OSS headquarters in Kunming after the war. John Alsop recommended me for a decoration, but after the war, he said, everyone returned home in such a harried fashion that his recommendation was probably overlooked. Never mind. The decoded, one-time-pad message that I received in the field from headquarters (*bottom*) I've always considered my decoration.

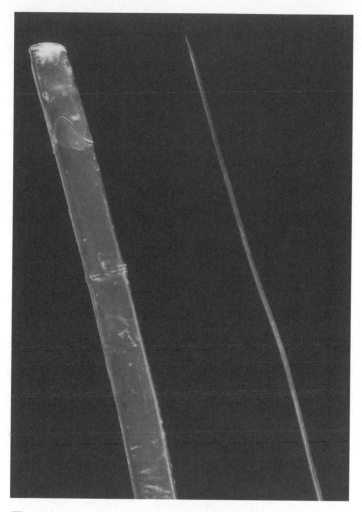

The midsection of the blade of this sword (*right*), which was given to me by Chinese military leaders, is bent. When I received it, some of the blade was caked in blood. I was told that the Japanese had used it to kill Chinese soldiers and civilians. I was puzzled how a sword as strong as this one could have been bent. Charles Normand, a military historian, examined it and said that it likely had been used in snapper work, such as tree felling, by the Japanese. They might have also used the sword as a big butcher knife (hence the blood). The leather-encased scabbard (*left*) is below the blade.

Several months before the end of the war, a Japanese plane made a crash landing near me. One of the survivors was a high-ranking Japanese officer who, although he walked away from the plane, shortly afterward committed suicide using his sword. Charles Normand notes that the sword was made by Tsuge, the great sword-making family of Japan.

Leave bundle of bandages at BAAG at
Hopo for Lt Alsops men.
Continue with Shin (courier) to
Hotien then send him on with following
instructions: With money
Change into plain clothes
at Hsintien and beware Nip sentries
at Henglung (Hypo 0610-2814) since
that point only short distance several
li from Nip defense line.
Proceed to Shihtouping (0604-2808)
Courier to wait at Yiki Inn at
SHIHTOUPING.

This hand-delivered, spook-speak message came to me from headquarters.
Lt. John Alsop was the leader of a small OSS group that spent about three
weeks not far from me engaged in successful skirmishes with the Japanese.
The BAAG (British Air Aid Group) was a covert political front. Its goal was
to help the British regain Hong Kong before the Nationalists arrived. So-
called defense lines changed every few weeks or even days. Headquarters
was unlikely to know of the actual location of the Japanese defense line
unless I had sent them the information—and I had not.

I was the guest of honor at a party given by Gen. Tong Pat about two months before the Japanese surrendered on the USS *Missouri*. In a scroll book each man at the party wrote a comment, which Shum followed with a translation. Here are two excerpts.

A rather pleasant-looking band of warriors (*left to right*): Shum Hay, guerrilla Colonel Chen, me, provincial magistrate Chai Cho Man, and Lung Chiu Wah. I believe this photograph was taken in Hotien a month or two before the war's end.

In 1982, Shum and his son David visited us in Boston. This photograph was taken at Logan Airport on their arrival from Canada. Shum died in Hong Kong a few months after his visit.

THE GODDAM
CHARLIE THREES

THE LONG VALLEY was a hazy sea in the early morning, with baby rice shoots rippling from the terraced waves; and the color of dawn was no different from the color of dusk. The air was cool and free of mosquitoes, and it was during this coolness that I got up each day and walked alone on the Ho-Po pathway to a certain point out of sight of the bridge. On this pathway men have traveled for almost two thousand years, in the small commerces of villages and in the lowly business of marching as soldiers. Men remember when Chiang Kai-shek led his soldiers on this path on their victorious march to Canton. If the Chinese were anxious to dot their countryside with plaques commemorating the passage of heroes, there would be, no doubt, many signs telling the traveler that the generalissimo had walked here, prayed in this shrine, attended vespers in that new church, defeated the enemy below that ridge, and, perhaps, slept in that farm house. In the early morning there tended to be a strip of fog browsing in the valley no higher than the slopes of the mountains, and when I was above the valley and looking down, the horizon seemed to be in the sky, the fog a beach on the earth.

On my outward trip there were never any wayfarers, but returning to Hotien I met groups of dejected farmers hopping along, always nearly off balance from the burdens of leafy greens and bamboo shoots that they hoped to sell for a good price in town. Seeing me, noticing the .45 on my hip, the lines of patience and weather became finer wrinkles about their eyes. The farmers smiled and wished me good morning, then quickened their hop-step into town, never looking back.

There was a cool spring on the side of the path where the mountain grew suddenly tall. Green foliage partly camouflaged the spring. I would nip a few leaves from a southernwood branch; they served as washrags, and I would rub them with the spring water against my face. But this spring was a stopping place on the return and I didn't stay there long. From the spring it was a short distance to a graveyard, and I walked there quickly. Blackened patches of hard-papered firecrackers littered the graves of those who had recently died. Sharp, brief sounds told of the ubiquitous presence of sparrows. They sped to other hills and valleys, and God was quiet. This vernal activity was a transparent one, emphasized by the emptiness that followed the passing of the birds and by the sight of the sleeping water buffaloes in the graveyard, silent with the eternity of the mountains and hills, with the watching of the gravestones and unswaying bamboo trees. I hurried back to the mission and went upstairs to the radio room.

There was a Japanese radio station in Shanghai which in the hours of early day had a program of music and chatter—an impassioned female voice sounded off in a hard flow of Japanese between mostly American records. She was probably the equivalent of an American disc jockey, and one of her favorite songs (it was not only the theme song of her program, and as such played at the beginning and end, but she liked it so much that she played it any number of times during the program) was also one of my favorites: "Over the Rainbow." I put the earphones on and turned the dials of the small, powerful radio, and usually I heard her clearly and without any airwave interruptions. "Somewhere over the rainbow" sang a hollow voice from a scratching needle on an old phonograph. With the earphones on, I turned myself sideways to the radio table and looked out one of the windows in the room, so small that you expected to find bars on it every time you looked. The mountains seemed to be dusting off a chalky greenness, ridges and rugged declines slowly appeared as though a negative were being developed into a fine print. I knew that about this time a young girl would be passing through the narrow alcove that separated the mission house from its church, where she helped Father Tan with his matins. I took off the earphones, went outside on the balcony to the end where I had my bed, and looked down over the balustrade. She came through the alcove, moving with the modest but curious grace of a swan. I smiled sleepily at her, and she knew that I would love to love her when she grew up. She put her brown fingers to the circular rim of her coolie hat, tipped her hat to one side, and glanced shyly up at me. She turned into the front courtyard, her body swaying, and walked around the middle part of the courtyard where there had been for several days a mound of rice from the last harvest drying in the sun. Then she entered the white church.

Letters from the States were bundled neatly on the table beside my radio. The edges of the letters resembled the airless folds of an accordion. Herbie the courier had brought eighteen letters on his last trip from headquarters. Daily I had been reading a letter from my girl, who was young and sweet to think of, and one from my mother, who, judging from the contents of her letters, spent her days following my collie-shepherd Duke everywhere and planting seeds of flowers in her garden.

I put the letters back in their bundle, then put the earphones on, and, yes, in a few minutes I heard the theme song of the Japanese station in Shanghai. This time it was played as the final theme of the program, and when the music stopped I put the earphones down and turned off the radio. Suddenly the shrill clanging from the three metalsmiths' stalls began: the day was beginning. In a few minutes Father Tan would ring the mission bell. I looked outside. The sun was rising gloriously on green maple trees huddled over canvas-brown homes.

"I'm going to sleep," I said, lying down again on my bed. "Give me a slight nudge when the war's over."

"Do not know *nudge*," Shum said.

I spent a clockful of time in bed each day, hoping and praying, issuing sacrilegious oaths, that the war would soon be over. The Japanese, during the month of June, gained leisurely ownership of the nearby hills, and it was difficult for us to locate unused hills to which we could run if they decided to come to Hotien. We didn't move anywhere, there was a paucity of intelligence about the enemy, and I was spending more and more time in bed. Shum's irritability seemed to grow with the month of June. One morning, in a particularly condemning mood of disgust, he came to my end of the balcony. "Don't be lazy," he said. "Get up. You will get sick if you stay in bed all the time."

"I'm already sick," I replied. "What do you want me to do, push-ups every morning?"

"Only woman who bears baby stays in bed as much as you. You will get bed sores."

"Do not know *bed sores*," I said.

The ceiling was solid and definitive, and I stared at it for a long, long time.

"Let's hungry," Shum said finally.

Food was a discouraging item, monotonous and unpalatable. My ambition was to change the main dish—rice. In my laziness it became even more abysmal. I had a poem clipped from an old magazine pasted on the wall in the radio room; substituting the word *dying* for *growing*, it read,

> *I'm dying, dying every day—*
> *Just watch how fast I do it.*
> *(Considering the food I eat,*
> *There's really nothing to it.)*

Our cook, Gee Dah, who had been a glove salesman before our arrival, showed a lack of imagination in the preparation of food: breakfast, rice and string beans; lunch, string beans and rice and small bugs; dinner, rice and string beans and large bugs. I wanted Shum to translate the poem into Chinese for the benefit, possibly for the amusement, of our cook, but he refused, for fear that Gee Dah would stop cooking. "Do not worry," said Shum. "There was a famine in this area one year ago."

There was a famine in everything except weather. The intelligence gathered from Jap-held towns was routine and not of much consequence. During June the Japanese seemed to be engaged in a track meet of sorts, with frequent messages informing us of troop movements between two coastal towns, Haifeng and Lukfeng, thirty-five kilos apart, with permanent garrison quarters in the middle schools of these towns. We encoded intelligence, or track meets, which Lung transmitted to headquarters. On 16 June: "Charlie Three. About three hundred Nip cavalry went to Haifeng from Lukfeng. Punch." Charlie Three meant that information had come from Chinese guerrillas; Punch was my code name. On 18 June: "Charlie Three. One hundred Nip infantry camouflaged with foliage will leave Haifeng tomorrow morning for Lukfeng. Punch."

On 22 June: "Baker Two. Three hundred and fifty Nip infantry and one hundred thirty-five cavalry arrived Haifeng yesterday from Lukfeng. Punch." Baker Two meant that my own agents had uncovered the information. Above Baker and Charlie came Able One; this meant that I myself had seen the origin of a report. That never happened.

The track meet gathered momentum as the days passed. The result of the Hai-Lukfeng relay was that a single P-51 flew out to the coast one day and strafed the course. The plane also dropped a couple of bombs, thus reducing the speed of the Japanese cavalry and infantry permanently since the two teams never bothered to repair the damage to the track.

Automobiles had not been invented as far as our area was concerned—there were no roads, much less railroad tracks. For about a month, shipping movements had been almost at a standstill. My Chinese agents were stationed in towns where the harbors were used by the Japanese Navy, and, as a result of their intelligence reports, more than five hundred Japanese had been killed in the bombing of a couple of small but overloaded vessels. The bombings, occurring about a month prior to the start of the Hai-Lukfeng race and lasting for a period of three spare weeks, had taught the Japanese not to go out on the water near us. Consequently, the agents spent less time on the waterfront and promontories south and north of the towns and began to congregate in tea shops, barbershops, and brothels, from which places they sent in rather contradictory messages.

Our urban agents sent us the following: "Five hundred and forty drums of gasoline and one hundred and fifty boxes of food moved into Catholic missions in Tung Kwan village of Matsung, waiting for sea-going vessel." A few days later another message came: "Still waiting for sea-going vessel."

The next information read, "Japs removed more than two hundred boxes of cannon shells from the Catholic mission in Tung Kwan Village." This information was given to headquarters, and a few days later General Tong reported that one of his agents discovered there was no Catholic mission in Tung Kwan Village. Are you sure? we asked him. Not sure, he answered.

We couldn't find the town on our maps. We decided to

send our best agents to find out what was up; Charlie Three, after a few days, said there was such a village but without a Catholic mission; Baker Two said the Catholic mission was no longer a mission because it had no priest for three weeks and, furthermore, a Jap colonel and two aides were keeping women in there; moreover, there was no gasoline, no food, and no ammunition.

This was confusing.

"I say to hell with it," I said to Shum one evening at supper.

"That is what I say, too," he said.

He was silent, eating his rice with an expression of pain, his cheeks puffed out like a hamster's. Suddenly he inhaled a tremendous wheeze of air, then gulped the food in a second. He put his chopsticks down, and looked at me rather sickly.

"You know what I think about agents?" he said.

"No," I replied.

He picked up a chopstick and pointed it at my nose. "This," he said. "We sent agents to town to get information. We give money for expenses in Jap town, but not for Hotien. Maybe they think that if there is nothing to give us, they will get fired, and have no job. So they stay in town and make up information. No good for us, but good for them."

I nodded.

"I have idea," Shum said. "We get agents to come back all the time from Jap towns on the coast. It is only a one-day trip if they start out in the morning and don't waste time. There is fish in the sea. Why can't agents bring fish with information they make up?"

Such an excellent plan should not go unrewarded, so I told Shum I was going to ask headquarters to increase his

salary. That night after supper I wrote a message to headquarters stating that interpreter Shum Wing's remarkable
efficiency should be acknowledged by a raise.

Soon the fish delivery was under way. Straw suitcases,
caddy sacks, newspapers, and certain types of enemy equipment held the fish for the fast-moving agents.

About a week into operation seafood, I received a message from headquarters concerning Shum's raise. "Cannot
meet your request of raise in salary for interpreter Shum.
Your judgment in variance with recent intelligence from your
station. Suggest you cut down on expenses." Had we been
without fish, this message would have made us downhearted.
But we forgot it as soon as it had been decoded and ate an
extra meal to show our lack of concern about the refusal.

Nevertheless, we began to worry a little about the intelligence reports. "This isn't so good," I told Shum gravely.
"Major Fletcher won't like this faulty intelligence. Especially
after our other mix-ups."

"It is bad," Shum said. "He thinks we don't know what
happens."

"We don't," I said.

"Most of the time we don't," he agreed. "You know what
I think?" he said. "We send no intelligence and just concen-
trate on having the agents get us fish. That way, no trouble
with headquarters, and we have good food."

Shum's proposal, warranting further praise, seemed to be
a deft solution to an aggravating situation, and we put it
into effect immediately. We accepted the agents' information,
thanked them and paid them, and ordered them to keep their
eyes open for superior catches of fish, and to try to step up the
speed of the deliveries; to retain the good taste, we told them,

it was necessary to arrive at Hotien before sundown because night somehow shed bad odors on un-iced seafood.

The shinfoo received a good bit of fish too. We always hoped to have a sufficient amount each day, enough to share with him.

The shinfoo appreciated our methods of gathering intelligence. "All right to kill fish," he would tell Shum upon receipt of a load of seafood. "This is how God wants you to act, and I approve. I will say special prayers for you. And by the way," he would often add, "some friends of mine are coming to visit me next weekend and I wonder if it might just be possible—at no danger to yourself, of course—to have your men bring about six or seven extra lobsters? My friends do not eat well and I want to surprise them."

One afternoon, while Shum and I walked a short distance on the path to Ho-Po for exercise, we saw Major Fletcher striding on a distant hill path, and Herb Wong, his unctuous interpreter with a dishonest face, was with him. Just in front were two coolies.

"My God!" Shum yelled. "What the hell?"

"I wonder what he wants," I said.

"Shall we hurry back to Hotien and hide?" Shum asked.

The major spotted us and waved for us to come meet him.

"We can't now," I told Shum. "Let's go meet the son of a bitch."

In about ten minutes we reached the party. "Hello, Major Fletcher," I said.

He pistoned out his hand like a revolver and I shook it.

"Hello, son," he said. He nodded to Shum.

Herb Wong stepped forward and bowed his head. He

raised it, but not much, so that I saw mostly his hair, and his ears, large and something like loud speakers. "You health, I hope," he said, rather timidly.

"Yours," I said.

We began walking, Major Fletcher and I leading Shum and Herb, but never quite catching up to the coolies who, despite the suitcases carried on yoke rods across the shoulders, jogged ahead at a considerable distance. They were practically running. Shum and Herb lagged behind us after a while.

"Put me up in the mission?" the major said.

"Yes, sir," I said. "There won't be room for your interpreter, though."

"That's all right. Don't need him. Can use yours."

"Yes, sir."

"Place for him to stay in this town?"

"Yes, sir, we can find him a room."

"Girls in the tea shops here?"

"No sir. Tea shops aren't worth a damn." I was about to mention the girl tea shops at Ho-Po, the town through which he had passed this morning, but decided against it, for Major Fletcher would probably want to know what I had been doing in Ho-Po when I was supposed to be in Hotien.

"Spent last night in Ho-Po. Superior girls working there." A smile widened lasciviously on his face, and after a minute or two of silence he reached in the hip pocket of his starched, dusty suntans, pulled out a checkered red handkerchief, and wiped his face. Next he took off his straw discus of a hat and wiped his head, and I noticed that his hair had thinned since the last time I had seen him, but there was still enough to form a mantle of sorts over the already bald part of the dome.

Except for the coolie hat, he wore American equipment, short trousers, shoes, and major's insignia.

The smile left his face as he balanced the hat on his head again. "Haven't been getting much intelligence from your station," he said. "Don't understand it. You had good stuff until recently. Did a lot of damage. Killed a jackpot of Nips," the major said.

"You did so much damage," I began, "that the Japs are not doing anything on the water and very little on land."

Major Fletcher said, "Not much going on around here, Pinck?"

"I think that's the situation," I said.

"You do? Hell, there's a goddam lot going on around here. Supposing there isn't, all the more reason for you to send correct intelligence."

"Yes, sir."

"Don't you check your agents?"

"We've been checking lately."

"The goddam Charlie Threes, how about 'em? God damndest junk I've ever read. Can't rely on Charlie Threes. How about 'em?"

"Until recently we didn't need to check them," I answered. "Their reports never contradicted ours."

We came near to the mission and I pointed to it.

"Huh," Fletcher said. "Stay overnight there. Get the hell back tomorrow. This Charlie Three commander, is he a good contact?"

"He doesn't seem to have many agents," I said. "And he stays pretty much in his farmhouse. That's the headquarters of the Chinese guerrillas, a few hundred yards from the town, by that mountain." I pointed toward the place.

Major Fletcher followed the direction but quickly looked back to the mission. "Contacts, Pinck," he said. "Contacts. I mean for business. What did he do before the war?"

"I don't know," I said, and I called to Shum and asked him if he knew what General Tong did before the war. He said that General Tong had been a general, he was sure. Taught military strategy at Whangpo Academy.

"Yes?" the major said, and waved to Shum, either thanking him or telling him to keep quiet.

"Wonder what he did to make a living?" Fletcher mused. "Some business. Musta been." He walked faster, and I had a hard time keeping up with him. Soon we crossed the bridge by the graveyard, two kilos from the mission. The sun was going down, and the mountains, blocking the valley in the west, sent ever more smoke-purple shadows funneling down the valley over the late afternoon mists of the paddy fields.

"Going to straighten this mess out, by God," he said as we walked into the compound of the mission. "Tell your interpreter to get word to that goddam Charlie Three to come here this evening. Want to leave in the morning. Want to see him tonight."

Shum and Herb came in the compound, and I told Shum to find a place for Herb to spend the night in town and, as soon as he finished that job, to go out to General Tong and tell him that Major Fletcher wanted to see him that evening. They left at once. The shinfoo came out in the courtyard and I introduced him to Fletcher. Father Tan spoke Chinese; the major growled English and said, in a loud aside, "What's this lord looking so happy about? He's the healthiest priest I've seen in China."

Lung poked his head out of the window of his first floor

room. I told him to tell Father Tan that we wanted Major
Fletcher to stay in the mission for one night and to ask him
if it was all right.

Lung said he wasn't dressed.

Ask him anyway, from where you are, I told him.

Lung strained his neck like a turtle and leaned farther
out the window. For a couple of minutes he and the shinfoo
exchanged sentences. The shinfoo waved his arms and ruffled
the skirt of his cassock.

"Shinfoo says all right," Lung said. "Shinfoo says he has
pleasure and wants to know if shrimp and lobster come
today."

I gulped and said with feigned indifference, "Oh, sure.
No matter. Of course."

"All right," Lung called. "Shinfoo has happy meals for
friends. Not fish for long time. They suffer from lack of
food."

Glancing at Major Fletcher, I saw that he was up in the
air and perhaps didn't even care to know what was going on.
He was rubbing his hands on his suntans and looking seriously at Father Tan and wonderingly at Lung, who puppeted
his head pleasantly from time to time at him.

Lung suddenly withdrew from the window. The shinfoo
and I took Fletcher to his room while a coolie brought his
suitcase.

"Want some water to wash up," he said, and after it had
been gotten, he added, "Rest now. See you for dinner. Got
much food here?"

"Rice and string beans," I answered, "three times a day."

"Jesus Christ," he said. He opened the suitcase; about

fifteen Army C-ration cans lined one side. "How's meat and vegetable stew?" he asked.

It had been lousy when I had last tasted it, on a troop train of the Great Indian Peninsula Railroad going from Bombay to Calcutta, but that was a year ago and I knew I would like it now. "Wonderful," I said.

He threw me three cans and said, "Cook 'em tonight. The padre eat with us?"

"No, sir."

"Here," Major Fletcher said, throwing me another can. "A present for him. My compliments."

When I left him I went to the radio room and prepared to make a weather report. I had to go outside for a few minutes, twirl the psychrometer and look at the sky. Lung was in the radio room, waiting to contact headquarters, counting a minute on his watch. I handed him the report, and he started the contact, signaling headquarters' call letters three times in succession, followed by our call letters twice; the procedure repeated itself four times, then Lung switched the set to receiving and put on the earphones. Headquarters heard him right away; he raised his hand and smiled mechanically to let me know.

He worked no longer than four minutes and was finished. I told him why Major Fletcher had come to see us. He asked no questions, and then I gave him the cans of meat and vegetable stew with instructions for Gee Dah the cook: put the cans in boiling water for five minutes or so; serve them in rice bowls; give one can to the shinfoo. Tell the shinfoo the fish was late today but would be here tonight, don't worry. Lung took the cans and hurried out.

Shum returned, looking worried.

"General Tong coming?" I said.

"Yes," he said in a tired voice. "The general will come after he has supper." Shum looked sad. "What you think?" he asked me, and proposed some alternatives to thinking of nothing. "Major Fletcher wants to give hell. Not to us, to General Tong. General Tong's not guilty. Nobody's fault. Cannot be helped, I say. But I don't want to see the general receive hell, and I don't want us to either. I think we should keep quiet."

Shum went on, "Say nothing. Major Fletcher blames the general more than us. If you say to him blame us and not the general, he probably won't do that, and will get us into trouble with him, more trouble than before. Only thing to do is let him blame General Tong. We don't speak."

The major displayed a unique sartorial personality, evidence of much primping, when he came out to the balcony for supper. Wearing an olive green necktie (an article we hadn't seen in months), he advertised the trig correctness of a military handbook model. He nodded perfunctorily to Shum and Lung and mounted a stool by the table. He said, "I'll be a son of a bitch, I'm hungry."

Gee Dah stood across from him, smiling solicitously.

Shum told Gee Dah we were ready to eat and to bring the food. The cook smiled in turn at each of us. Then he walked ceremoniously away, was gone only a minute, and reappeared carrying four rice bowls in which cylindrical headstones of C-ration cans were buried in mounds of rice.

Major Fletcher said, "Jesus Christ," and gaped.

Shum, who was always susceptible to phrases, repeated, "Jesus Christ."

Lung picked up his chopsticks and nibbled some rice around his can. "Rice is good," he said emphatically.

"Tell Gee Dah to open the goddam cans," I said to Shum.

"Jesus Christ," the major repeated.

We finished supper.

That evening the major and I sat on the balcony. "It's easy to understand why your intelligence is fubared," Major Fletcher said sternly, "but this is a serious business you're in."

"Yes sir," I said.

"Try to run this goddam place better. Check up on things, everything. Need your station. Valuable to us." He tried a smile, and spoke in a more or less forgiving voice. "These goddam Charlie Threes, got to check on them. This Tong guy, be here soon?"

"Soon as he eats," I answered, feeling rather guilty because I knew General Tong wasn't going to be happy talking to the major. I wished I had been able to tell him to leave Hotien for a day.

Father Tan appeared in the doorway of the balcony, smiling. He spoke to Shum.

"Major Fletcher," Shum said, "Father Tan has thanks for can of meat. A blessing, he calls it. Father Tan will say special prayers for you."

"Have him join us," said the major.

"Shinfoo says yes, for a few minutes. Friends coming soon," Shum said.

"Tell him to sit down."

Father Tan sat down by the railing along the balcony. Frequently he turned away to look down into the courtyard. When he wasn't looking over the railing, he was sipping a cup of tea, which the cook repeatedly filled when he turned his back to look.

Suddenly the shinfoo stood up and waved his hands, leaning far over the railing. In a high voice he talked to someone in the courtyard. A Chinese voice chopped back at him. Lung stood up, looked over the side, and said happily, "Fish here, fish here! Two suitcases full."

Lung and the shinfoo turned to us, talking to each other. The agent with the fish came upstairs to the balcony; he bowed until Shum told him to stop. Then he put the straw suitcases, fuming with the smell of fish, on the table and opened them. Father Tan spoke to Shum, clapped his hands, and picked out seven lobsters from the suitcase.

"What's this?" Major Fletcher asked.

"Oh," I answered carelessly, "this is just fish."

"Where did it come from?"

"The coast. Not far."

"Who's this Charlie?"

I shrugged. "A friend," I said.

I wanted to tell Lung to speak Chinese, if he had to speak at all, and I had just decided to get him inside and away from the major when he suddenly brightened into a condescending smile and said, pointing to the agent with the fish, "Ah, no, this man says we owe him money for last two trips, and he says his friend Ah Chung needs ten thousand more dollars for best operations. No news about Japs. Intell—" Like a jack-in-the-box he shot up with a scream of confusion and pain. "God damn, Shum, what you kick—" Shum stopped him again with another boot under the table and cannoned him with Chinese.

"Jesus Christ!" Major Fletcher roared.

Father Tan smiled benignly and crossed himself.

"I'll be a son of a bitch," the major said. "What the hell goes on here?"

At this point there was only one thing to do and that was to tell him the truth. So I told him part of the truth. I said we arranged for infrequent deliveries of seafood. For example, when an agent had to come back to Hotien to receive secret instructions and when he needed money and had no news of importance (that is, no news at all), well, to bring us some fish certainly elevated our morale and kept us healthy. Besides making the best use of our agents, we always gave some to our Chinese friends for close cooperation, and what was there to lose?

Major Fletcher told me. He took a rather realistic view of our predicament and, much to my surprise, said it was all right for the agents to buy seafood and bring it to us as long as they didn't spend too much money. He was still displeased with the intelligence and he lectured on what was wrong and what might be done to correct it. The greatest blame remained ominously over the bald head of General Tong.

Father Tan had retired for the night, and we were drinking tea when the general arrived at the mission. He saw our kerosene lamp and greeted us from the courtyard. Shum and I were happy to see him and told him to come up and have tea. The course that the major was going to take didn't come as a shock, for we knew he had it in for the general, but we were surprised and downhearted when he said, "Tell that son of a bitch to get the hell up here. Can't wait all night." Sadly Shum and I looked at each other.

General Tong strode onto the balcony, saluted us in an unmilitary, friendly way, and started to speak to Shum but was interrupted by the major's baritone. "Tell that goddam Charlie Three I'd like to know what the hell's happened to his goddam intelligence," he said.

Shum looked at the major and said nothing.

"All right," the major said, "tell him. You speakee Chinee?"

Shum stared at him a minute longer and then turned his head to General Tong, smiling. He spoke courteously, and occasionally the general and he laughed. I wondered what they were laughing about.

"Major Fletcher," Shum said flatly, "General Tong wishes to pay his respect to you and regrets that his intelligence has not been good. He is at fault, he said, because he has not kept the strictest watch over his agents. Many of his good agents have left him because there was no money to pay them."

"Ask him what the hell he's doing about it."

Major Fletcher didn't ask General Tong to sit down.

The general stood by the table, like a relaxed prisoner at the bar; he didn't appear in the least agitated by the outbursts. His thumbs caught hold of the inside of his wide belt. The general was short, lean, and tough; he had been on the carpet before higher officers than the major, and it seemed to me that he had decided not to let this calling-down ruffle his pleasant composure.

"The general says he will check his information. Unless he is sure of what agents tell him, he will not give us any information."

"Hell," the major said, "how's he going to do it?"

"General Tong says he will send two agents to check what one agent reports."

"How can he do that? He's short of agents."

"General says he will find way. To the sincere utmost he will get correctness. He appreciates what America does to help his country. He and his guerrillas offer you congratulations and good wishes for your work in helping to win the war. He hates Japs with his heart."

General Tong must have looked too much at ease to suit the major. Once during the interrogation, while Shum and the general were talking, the general suddenly chuckled and cuffed me comradely on the shoulder. I wondered what the hell he was so happy about. Major Fletcher indicated by his look that he was going to try a sarcastic frontal attack.

"Does the Charlie know that the chief rivers in his country run east and west and that they never run that way in other countries? Christ, I bet he doesn't know his name or rank or serial number or what his job is or his middle initial. Can't win this goddam war with him."

"General Tong says yes, that is something he learns in school at early age. There are many unusual geologies in China. He commends you on your knowledge."

Major Fletcher was red in the face. "Went to school?" he said disbelievingly. "I luh. Taught at Whangpo. Know Chiang?"

"The general regrets that he does not know Chiang Kai-shek, George Washington of China."

"I'll be a son of a bitch," the major said. "This Charlie have a business?"

"General Tong says war is his business. Hopes to have success."

Lethargy overcame Major Fletcher. Pointing to a stool, he invited General Tong to sit down, which he did with a grateful look at Shum and me. Then Shum and I sat down on either side of the major, and for an hour the major discussed in a low voice ways and means of improving our intelligence. He was very civil and talked from a warehouse of technical information, some of which I understood, some of which I listened to. But I was unhappy thinking of his discourteous manner to my friend General Tong. Twice the major asked me questions and I had to ask him to repeat them because I was thinking of his rudeness. The second time he bounded back into his usual world, but instead of getting mad at me, he started cursing the general ("that goddam Charlie Three with no business") and wondered aloud how he would ever win the war with such intelligence as he was getting from the Chinese in general and Tong in particular.

"Going to bed," the major said abruptly. "'Night to this gent. Leaving in the morning, early morning when it's dark." He stood up, looked contemptuously at General Tong, jerked his head to signify the end of the meeting, and went inside to his room.

I felt awful. Shum and General Tong were laughing softly, and that made me feel even worse as I didn't see any reason for laughing. So I stared dully out past the mission at the valley and the mountains and tried to think of something considerate to say to the general. There was nothing to say.

Shum and Tong toasted each other with tea, laughing and smiling. The general slapped me on my back and put out his other hand toward Shum, motioning him to speak to me.

"General Tong says we drink to success," Shum said enthusiastically. "Have *gombei* pretty soon to celebrate approaching victory over little cucumber bastards." (*Gombei* meant "bottoms up.")

"What are you so happy about?" I asked.

"War ends soon, maybe. Rejoice for victory."

"Aw, hell, this is no time to be so goddam happy."

"Yes. Fine time."

Shum and the general spoke for a long while, changing the conversational rhythm numerous times but never losing their happy tone.

"Shum," I asked stupidly, "why are you two so happy?"

"Why not?" he said.

I said I felt awful because the major had given General Tong hell.

Shum looked hard at me a second, then a wide, knowing grin spread across his face. "Ah," he said, "You don't know. Major Fletcher didn't give General Tong hell. No. Never."

"I heard him," I said gruffly.

"Ah, no. I tell General Tong not what he says to tell him. Don't worry."

"What did you tell him?" I asked Shum.

"I tell General Tong that major is deaf and has to talk loud, not to mind his voice." Shum paused to drink a toast with the general, then continued. "I tell him Major Fletcher comes here to tell us what good job we are doing, all of us, and that he hopes, but doesn't see how, we will do even better job of getting ahead of the Japs. The major appreciates his efforts and will try to get him some American guns and ammunition." The general winged his arms on both our shoulders and Shum continued, "Everything is all right. I just ask General Tong to have supper with us tomorrow. He says the lobster look very good, and he will be pleased to come."

7

FIND THE
CHINESE DOCTOR

WHEN SHUM got back from an overnight trip to Ho-Po, where he investigated reports of Japanese agents nesting in local stores, the first thing he said was, "I have a great sickness in me. I am sick, my fever was high in Ho-Po before I left, and I do not know what it is. I would rather be sick here. I must go to bed now."

Lung and I helped him upstairs, and we set up a bed in the radio room with double layers of white mosquito netting. Lung took off Shum's clothing and spread a sheet and blanket over him. His eyes, barely open, were all black and muddied.

I got a glass of water and put it to his mouth. He couldn't

swallow. "Malaria, Shum," I said. "You've got to take some atabrine."

"No chill. Just fever," he said, putting his hands behind his head. He was very tense. "I don't know. Aspirin. My head hurts."

Lung dipped some towels in a bucket of water and put the wet towels around Shum's head. In a few minutes Shum closed his eyes and seemed to be sleeping.

On the balcony Lung said that he thought Shum was very sick with one of the nameless fevers that frighten people in Southeast Asia, not malaria. Nobody knew what caused the fevers or what they were. The word "fever" included many diseases, and many people died from the fever. Iodine, pro-kits, atabrine, Band-aids, and sulfadiazine didn't help all diseases; men behind the lines suffered from their distance from doctors. There was the story of the British agent who walked three days with a ruptured appendix to the nearest doctor and the story of an American agent whose interpreter was refused help by a German doctor living in the same town on the refugee route north from Canton because the agent happened to be Jewish. (With the help of his .45, the agent persuaded the German to operate on his interpreter, the American hold-ing the pistol as the German used his scalpel.) Such incidents were troublesome to the mind that rejected the possibility of getting sick, or being captured, or killing friendly Chinese through erroneous target information. The stories, whenever I thought about them, had, after all, happened to someone else.

"Dammit, Lung, he's got malaria."

Lung shook his head. "No," he said firmly. "You can tell

malaria, we all get it. Fever. Chill. Cold and hot, always cold and hot. Shum is sick from other sickness."

I told him he was wrong.

He shook his head vigorously and looked out at night shading up the valley and cutting down the mountains. "That's wrong," he said. "I am right, I know why I talk." Lung was curiously proficient in English when there was a crisis. He walked over to the window in the radio room, looked in for a second, his face caught in the dull oil light, and came back. "No," he began once more, "Shum is very sick, and I shall go into town and find the man who knows medicine."

I told him he was as wrong as could be, nobody in Hotien knew medicine.

"No. There is man who runs shop where malaria medicine is in front with other pills. He studied nursing and nursed an Englishman in Hong Kong for two years before he died. I know him and think him fine man. Good guy. Play poker with him for many stakes. He never wins. Fine man." Lung shuffled the distance from the door to the balustrade, looking hopefully at me for confirmation of his recommendation. "Knows medicine," he added.

"He really studied nursing?" I asked.

"Yes. Shum knows him. They talk medicine when I meet them, at shop."

"You think we should have him look at Shum?"

He said he did.

A tall, slow man with an austere face and bony hands preceded Lung up the stairs. He stared coolly at me, then bowed slowly and rose. He opened his hands like a phlegmatic preacher praying for rain in the Bible belt. *Now lead me to the sick man,* I translated his silence. *I will treat him with my skill, and the evil fever will disappear.*

In the radio room, he glided to Shum and peered through the mosquito netting, his face covered with a medically contemplative mask. He spoke in Chinese.

"A sick man, he says," Lung announced. "That's no news to us," he said confidentially, "but this man knows his medicine and by that he means to say we were not wrong in sending for him. This man says Shum is a sick man. It is not malaria."

"What is it? Ask him."

"He says, for sure he doesn't know, but thinks maybe it is a local fever. Has seen it many times before."

Shum groaned.

"Ask him how he can tell anything, just standing like a dummy," I said. "Christ, you can hardly see Shum through the netting."

"This man says you don't know medicine. Man who has to tap on patient's head, knock on chest, look in eyes, is not skilled doctor. He says he is skilled in local disease. Knows them all, but doesn't know the name for some." Lung scratched his head. "He says he will know in while what is the sickness and already has the treatment for it in his pocket."

A low groan fogged out from the white netting.

It was humid and awfully hot, and I felt grimy vapors seeping through the netting's pores.

"Easy, Shum," I said, half-believing myself, "you'll be all right. Easy does it." I changed the wet towel and asked him how he felt. "Aw, hell," he answered feebly.

The man jammed his hand within his blouse and took

out an ampule of yellow fluid and put it on the table. Again his hand disappeared, and this time it came out holding a syringe with a very long needle. He picked up the ampule and plunged the needle through its cap.

Shum's voice moaned from the bed. "Goddam crazy fool. He's putting air in the serum. Make him draw the air out before he puts it in me."

I remembered that was something doctors always did.

"Give it to me," Shum said with great effort. "I'll do it."

Lung took the instrument and gave it to Shum.

"I can't tell," he said as he gave it back to Lung. Shum put his hands behind his head, grinned with an effort, and pronounced that he would die.

"Ask the man what's wrong," I said.

Lung said, "Does not know. Says Shum is sick. Local fever."

"What the hell's he giving him?" I asked.

"Cure."

"Cure for what?"

"He says he doesn't know name of fever for sure. It is a local fever and this serum cures local fevers. He brought many of this cure with him from Hong Kong. To save lives here. Sure cure, he says, on memory of relative dead three hundred years and a great surgeon."

"All right, tell him to go ahead."

When Lung finished speaking, the man turned his back to us, pursed his lips with disdain, and folded his hands tightly. He stood tall and quiet and didn't seem wearied by the heat.

"What's wrong with him?" I asked Lung, pointing to the doctor.

"He received offense. Says we think he does not know medicine. He says he knows plenty medicine." Lung spoke loudly, as if he were trying to proclaim the stupidity of the doctor.

"Tell him we think he knows plenty medicine, we just didn't want him to kill Shum."

Lung smiled approvingly. He grinned at Shum, who was moaning again, and said benevolently, "Shut up. You'll be all right. This man is real doctor: no knocking on head, no tapping on chest. Real doctor."

Shum answered, "Aw, hell."

The local doctor reached in the netting and pulled at Shum's arm, and I would have sworn that his eyes were closed when he jabbed the needle in. The serum went in slowly, as though the doctor himself feared the injection. Finished, he examined the syringe, pumped it a few times, swished it in the air, then took it apart and put the pieces back in his blouse. He stepped back, bowed to each of us, including Shum, and spoke to Lung.

"Money," Lung said. "Money he wants. Maybe four thousand."

"Tell him we'll pay him as soon as Shum's all right."

Shum groaned.

The doctor left, despair at our condition of payment having erased his composure. "Not so, not so," was what he told Lung in protest. We turned the lamp's wick down, leaving a flicker of light, and waited by the bed for Shum to get well.

Shum fell asleep after a while, and Lung suggested that I go to bed while he watched for any change. So I went out on the balcony and went to sleep.

"Get up. Quickly!" I turned over on my back. "Get up!"

I mumbled, asking what the trouble was.

"Shum tried to shoot himself," Lung said. "He reached for his gun in his holster. I stopped him."

I got out of bed, fully awake, and went to the radio room.

"Shum, what's the matter? For God's sake."

Shum lay prone on the bed, his left arm scraping the floor. The muscles in his neck bunched in purple streaks.

We turned him over and applied some fresh wet towels to his head and face. Lung said, "Too much pain. He hurts terrible. Shum said he must not stand it more. He reached for his gun but I stopped him."

I turned the lamp brighter. The mosquito netting hung open in the middle like a stage curtain, and I pushed it farther apart. Shum gripped his right forearm suddenly. "What's wrong, Shum?" I asked.

He grunted in pain and slid his grip down. "Goodbye," he said.

"Goodbye. What do you mean goodbye? You aren't going anywhere."

"I am dying. Now goodbye. The goddam fool gave me a drug for warts or malaria. I do not have malaria. Maybe it has poison reaction to disease."

"You were a medical student. Don't you have any idea what's wrong?"

"Too great fever. Maybe it is air."

"Nonsense."

Shum closed his eyes.

"I make Shum promise not to shoot himself," Lung said as he began to wipe Shum's forehead.

"Where's the gun?" I asked.

"No, no," Shum whispered. "I will not shoot myself. It

was the great fever. My mind was out of me. I do not care for the gun. I promise. I will try to live. Lung took it."

"I put it on the balcony when I came to get you," Lung said.

"Leave it there. Ah, this kills me. The fool, fool." Shum changed to Chinese, moaning and cursing.

Ten minutes passed. "Chinese doctor," Shum said. "Get me a Chinese doctor. They know what to do." He turned over and let his left arm unlock to the floor. "He will know."

"Shum," I said, "you don't want the Chinese doctor. He's no doctor."

"He's no doctor with school training, but he knows many diseases that trained doctors don't know," Shum said.

"How can he get you well?"

"I don't know," he answered.

"Nursing almost killed you."

"Bastard."

"So's the Chinese doctor," I said.

"No," Shum said. "In China the old Chinese medicine men are like country doctors in America. We read about American doctors in school."

"All right," I said. "If you want him, we'll send for him. Good luck."

"Okay," Shum said with emphasis.

I asked Lung if he could find the Chinese doctor in town. "Ah," he replied, sitting down on the edge of the bed, "that is good idea. Chinese doctor gives Chinese medicine." He crossed his legs. "Yes, Chinese medicine. I'll go find him now." He got up and went to the door, turned back for a tired glance, and told Shum not to worry. Shum mouthed four letters, and after Lung had gone he smiled and promised that the old Chinese doctor would make him well. The Chinese doctor was trained in Chinese medicine, different from serums and sulfas and Band-aids, Shum said thoughtfully. In a few minutes he closed his eyes and breathed like a man sleeping, though I didn't think he was. I wiped the sweat off my face and neck with the mosquito netting, then went to the radio table and straightened the articles on it. Iodine. Band-aids. Sulfadiazine. Atabrine. There wasn't much sulfadiazine left. Didn't have but a platter of twenty pills when we came in the field. Four left. Nuts.

The Chinese doctor startled me. He hopped into the room flopping his arms like a bat. He was about five feet tall and wore a halo of gray hair around a bronzed, cooper-shining dome. His eyebrows were gray too. His nose was turned up, and he had a smile over his whole face. Laugh lines of wrinkles crowfooted brightly around his eyes. He was maybe seventy years old, and his brown suit was wearing thin at the elbows and knees.

Shum smiled when he saw him.

The Chinese doctor had a soothing voice. Though he didn't have a watch, he took Shum's pulse. He came back to the pulse quite a few times and seemed to know exactly what he was doing. He looked at Shum's eyes and muttered "Ha," paused, then muttered again, "Ha." It sounded very professional. The doctor was a Chinese leprechaun.

"The doctor says Shum is very sick," Lung said, and added a moment later, "Good doctor."

Shum lay sweating and breathing heavily as though he had a pile of bricks on his chest.

"Shum's awfully sick," I said aloud, thinking to myself if

he died it would be my fault, I would have to get word to his parents, and headquarters would probably put the blame on me. Selfish thoughts, I knew, but I couldn't avoid considering these sorrows and stupidities, which traveled together like birds wheeling in unison in a windless sky to fan air on each other. In imagining the consequences, Shum's death was almost forgotten.

I put my hands on Lung's shoulder. "Lung," I said, "tell the doctor I'll give him twenty thousand dollars to get Shum well."

Lung grinned cowishly. "No, no," he said, shrugging away my hand. "Not necessary. Never earns that much money. No. He doesn't need that much money. Shum will get well."

Twenty thousand dollars exceeded Lung's monthly salary. "No, Lung," I said in a voice that I hoped would carry an inflexible will. "Tell him what I told you."

He laughed and said I was crazy, maybe sick, and put his hand on my forehead.

"Tell him."

Lung talked to the Chinese doctor. I wondered whether he was telling him about the money. The doctor recognized Lung's final silence by grabbing both of Shum's wrists and searching for and finding the pulses. A song of Chinese rolled off his tongue. "Oh boy oh boy oh boy" was what he seemed to be singing.

Lung closed his eyes and shook his head with delirious speed, like a wet dog shaking himself. "God," he grunted, then stopped, looking at me with a weird expression. "You know this Chinese doctor is a good man. He knows Chinese medicine, and I think Shum get well. You give him too much money. He says so himself, but will accept it, and says he realizes you have a kind heart and will always remember you. To get Shum well he says he would have got in Shum's fever himself."

"That's what I want to know."

"He says he will go downstairs and prepare some broths with special herbs in them to take away the fever."

Watching the Chinese doctor was a new experience. His knowledge of medicine skirted time, and he moved to the usual chest tappings dispassionately and humorously, occasionally slapping lightning bugs on his face and skull and laughing with a surprising rumble when successful. He massaged Shum's arm; at times he held it perfectly still in a loose grip, blowing on it.

Footsteps marked time in the room. I turned to face the other end. Standing in the doorway, his body rigid with scorn and dignity, was the medicine man who had studied nursing.

The Chinese doctor saw him and whistled. Perhaps to drive him away.

The nurse spoke directly to Lung, ignoring his competitor.

"Old bastard wants to know if cure has worked yet," said Lung, standing erect like a cadet. "'Go to hell,' I tell him. Has sick family to take care of. Needs money now. 'Almost twelve o'clock,' he says. 'Shum should be up now.' I order him to go back to his goddam shop and to go to sleep. 'Take care of dead people,' I say."

"Yes," I said. "Good advice."

Lung nodded. "Ha," he said, "I think good medicine for

him is shooting." He about-faced and shouted at the nurse, who took it for a sentence or two then went out of the radio room, thumping on the stairs.

A sudden wind pushed the mission's bell in faint tapping sounds that carried no echoes. The sound and smell of death came into the mission. The moon had passed the halfway mark of night and now lofted into the darkest part of the sky, fading then twinkling like a transport's navigation light.

"This man say Shum will get well. Be back with broths and herbs."

"Oh boy oh boy oh boy," the Chinese doctor seemed to be saying.

I thought about the moon and how I had learned to tell the time, within half an hour or so, by its position. At the window I saw the moon and guessed it was 2:45; then I looked at my watch: it was only 1:45. I was way off.

The Chinese doctor left and returned in a few minutes carrying two kettles that perked out steam and the smell of chicken broth. He set the kettle on the radio table beside our medical supplies and, reading my thoughts from the corner of his eye, put his face to the mouth of the kettle and inhaled. A simple smile spread over his face.

"Good things in the broth. Chinese herbs and old medicine and an old chicken. He keeps three chickens in his house always for emergency like this. He said maybe if you get sick he get you some broth," Lung said, looking enviously as the doctor poured some into a bowl.

I asked him if that was a promise.

"He says you bet your life."

The old man padded across the floor to the bed. Raising

Shum's head to the crook of a rest in his arm, he slipped the broth, overflowing slightly into two brown moustaches of fluid, into his mouth. Shum tried to smile.

"Lucky fellow," I said, "you *won't* get well if you have that every day. I told the doctor I might get sick myself, just to get some of the broth. There's chicken in it."

The doctor, wiping Shum's mouth dry with his coat sleeve, looked up and nodded confidently.

He went back to the radio table, set the bowl down, and looked with what may have been forced surprise at our collection of medical supplies. He picked up the bottle of iodine, shook it a couple of times, and studied it near the lamp. The old man examined all the articles, talking to Lung as he inspected each one. Then he went to the bed and looked around the room. Lung gave him a chair.

"This man say we can go, how you say it? hit the sack," Lung said. "No need to worry, he will stay here all night and look at Shum each minute."

Somehow I had confidence in the old man. Perhaps I was too impressed by a person's manner, but always, and often successfully, I have transferred a man's common bearing into a measure of his professional merit. No matter that he treated his patients with herbs; chicken broth, I remembered, was a staple for the sick back home in the South. All right, we would let him stay with Shum the rest of the night. Treat him with his Chinese medicine.

"Okay, okay," Lung said impatiently. "He says take off. He knows what to do and will do it. Find well man in the morning. Old Chinese doctor knows the stuff. Okay?"

I hoped it would be.

It was hard going to sleep again. I lay awake a long time,

and when I opened my eyes in the morning the sun was winking over the rim of a mountain. A pleasant sight, I thought,
tracing the various patterns of shade on the mountains cup-
ping the valley. I might learn how to tell the time of day by
the position of the shadows. I got up, dressed, and threw cold
water on my face. The mission was still sleeping, and below
the balcony the center courtyard was hard and yellow, with
still-wet fringes of grass encroaching in untidy streaks upon
the rectangle of cement. Daily, the grass made a little progress; the gentle rains helped. By the far end of the balcony
the curtain-netting on the radio room rustled in slow down-
ward flutes.

The old man got up as I came in; smiling, he pointed to
Shum, who was sleeping easily. He took my hand and put it
on Shum's forehead, telling me, in his own way, that the fever,
or the highest degrees of it, had disappeared. Watching me
intently, he recognized my discovery of his success, and then
the simple smile widened over his face. Still holding my hand,
he lifted it off Shum's forehead and, standing beside the bed,
like two long-lost brothers, we pumped each other's hands,
way up, way down. The little old Chinese doctor pointed to
the kettles and said, evidently in praise of the contents, "Dıng
Hao, ding hao."

I answered, "You're damn right, Doc."

We sat around and smiled for perhaps fifteen minutes,
the old man grinning proudly and I respectfully. "You're all
right, Doc," I said. "Damn fine medicine man!"

Lung came in, sleepy-eyed and dusty, wearing his wrinkled black suit; the old man motioned to him and they spoke
a while in quiet voices by the radio table.

"What's up, Lung?" I asked.

Lung spread his arms and mumbled something in Chinese. He went to Shum and looked at him. Then he called to the old man, who came over to the bed. Lung snapped his fingers, by habit, and he and the doctor stood there talking. I went to the radio table and sat down on a stool. The smell of chicken broth hung in that part of the room. Reaching for the kettle to see if any was left, I noticed the medical supplies: iodine, Band-aids, and sulfadiazine—but the plastic platter for the sulfa tablets was empty. I was sure I had seen the last four there before I went to bed. I picked up the platter and shook it. Nothing jiggled. The sulfadiazine tablets were gone. Carefully I glanced at Lung and the old Chinese doctor. Hell, we could have dosed Shum with sulfa ourselves, why call a goofy old man who was supposed to know Chinese medicine to use broths and mysterious herbs? And why pay him twenty thousand dollars to use our medicine? "Lung," I said, "come here. What the hell do you call this?" Lung dropped away from the old man and came over to the radio table. I pointed to the sulfadiazine platter. "What the hell?" I asked. "Chinese medicine, my foot!"

Lung repeated, "Your foot?"

"Goddam," I said. "The old bastard gave him our sulfa! What do you call that?"

Lung closed his eyes; he turned and opened one eye on me and answered in Chinese.

"Crap, Lung," I said, trying desperately to interrupt him and failing. Chinese rolled out temperately, and he accepted my outburst with equanimity, if not plain selfish unconcern. Each time I spoke, he continued to speak Chinese. "Aw, hell," I said softly. "You speak English!" For a second Lung grinned. He raised his arm, pointing to the bed, and droningly lapsed into a current of Chinese. I was almost to the saturation point when I glanced at Shum, who lay in a feverless, easy sleep. He was going to recover; the thoughts of the night seemed foolish, somehow, now that he was not going to die. Then I realized that Lung's stubbornness, his refusal to speak English, signified the end of another crisis.

"Ding hao," I said.

"B'd'ung," Lung said, indicating he did not understand me.

The Chinese doctor whistled a trill. "Oh boy oh boy oh boy," he seemed to be saying.

MAYBE THEY'RE
JAPS

STANDING JUST off the single paved street of Hotien, in a narrow, wooden-sided store with a dark-pounded earth floor, I watched the heat of the day zoom from the shade down into the street, where the pavement ended, over a maple tree spreading deferentially over people talking in its shade. A parched old man came out of a house near the tree and took his place in the sun, his pipe wreathing smoke in the green-gold sunlight. Old men had their place in the sun; they sat and watched and spoke to travelers bringing a parcel of news. Everyone respected them, these old men, the elder statesmen who contented themselves with the smiles and good humor of things eternal. The sun was their friend and sustained them. The old men waved lazily. Some storekeepers hadn't yet opened their shops, some were removing sections of wood from the front of the stores, the doors that didn't exist during the day. The business of buying a chop (an official stamp), with Shum as my interpreter, was going along rather casually; the chop man didn't mind my wandering from the shop and into the street. The progress of the sun up the main street was a sight I liked to see. The chop man followed me to the front of his shop and held up two blocks of wood, one black and smooth, one brown and grained with darker lines. "Both good wood," Shum said. "The man says both same, no difference in world. You can see that. You choose."

"The black one."

"The chop man says black wood dependable."

"Good."

"When do you want it?"

"Tomorrow."

"He says he will have job tomorrow. Dependable is his password."

"Magnificent," I said.

"Do not know *magnificent*."

"Great, then."

"Oh. Great. Thank you."

"You forget any words when you were sick?"

"No, I don't think so."

"Great," I said.

"Do not know *great*." Shum smiled and adjusted his shoulder holster.

I said, "Magnificent. Why don't you tie the piece of leather on your pistol to your holster or one of the straps?"

"I don't know," he answered. "What's it for?"

"Keeps your pistol. You won't lose it."

"Oh?" he said. He took a comb from his shirt pocket and combed his hair. "That I didn't know."

"You know it now," I said.

"That's true."

"Yes, it's true."

"Chop tomorrow?"

"Right."

"Ho!" he snorted. "Yes!"

"The chop man says will we come in back of shop where he will design address and name and title for chop." Shum started in. "What do you want to put on it?"

"Oh. Address, name, title," I said. "My name, Shum, and let's put down Hotien for the address; everyone, including ten million Japs, knows that we stay in the Catholic mission. For a title, let's have Fourteenth Air Force; everyone knows the Flying Tigers." A new chop seemed in order for the documents we sent to General Tong and our agents; the old chop blurred when rubbed in the red ink pad of cotton, the characters had not been chiselled deeply.

"The chop man says that's many characters to put on a small chop."

"Yes," I said. "Tell him I think so, too."

Shum and the chop man huddled over the counter, drawing Chinese characters.

A woman came in from the yard in the back and went directly to a low, round stool by the counter. Presently, a baby with scabs on its face and legs toddled to her. She lifted it to her lap, and opened her blouse, glaring sulkily at the chop man, Shum, and me. The baby grabbed at her breast like a monkey. Her face was so serious in its scorn that I must have stared at her. As I turned, I saw two monstrous Asians, well over six feet tall, staring at me from outside the shop. I hadn't seen them in Hotien before. I looked at their feet: wide square spaces in between the big toes and the next. I remembered learning about the size of Japanese feet in a *Terry and the Pirates* comic strip. They wore coolie pants, blue and torn. I slowly put my hand on my .45. The monsters noticed. I walked to the street. They walked away. Near the end of the street they went into a bicycle shop.

"Shum," I called hoarsely. I pointed to the bicycle shop and told him what I had seen.

The shop was open-fronted and walled with clay and timber beams. Not many bicycles, some with the wheels off, stood against the walls. A boy was repairing the spokes in a rusty wheel. We stood outside and looked at the giants, who now stared dully at the earth floor.

Shum's morning drowsiness shot into nervousness. He pulled at my arm. "I see," he said, "I think never mind."

"Maybe they're Japs."

"No, no. Not Japs, Dan, Chinese. Big Chinese, you know?"

"Look at their feet," I said.

He looked. The big Asians must have known what I was thinking. I put my hand on my .45, and they continued to look at the floor as though they were now looking at their feet, too.

"No," Shum said, decisively. "Big Chinese, Dan. You know, big Chinese? Many wear same sandals, make space beside big toe. Cannot tell Jap that way." He laughed. "Let's go to tea shop. Time for tea. Refreshing."

General Wu was sitting in the tea shop, alone, at the

round table on the second floor, sipping steaming tea and nibbling poppyseed cakes. We yawned at one another. What the hell were we doing up so early? He poured some tea for us. "Shum, tell General Wu about the Japs."

"They are not Japs," he protested.

"All right," I said. "Tell him about the big Chinese."

They conversed in their language. Then Shum said that General Wu thought I might be right. Would I like to go shooting in the afternoon at the bicycle shop? I said I certainly would, and we made an appointment to go shooting after lunch. We drank our tea, and after a few remarks on the weather and the unequal distribution of land in China, we left General Wu and returned to the mission.

At lunch, before we finished eating the rice and string beans, a messenger came from General Wu telling us that the general was not able to go shooting in the afternoon. "This fellow," said Shum, "comes here with evil news. General Wu has boils that cause him great pain. He thinks he ate too many cakes this morning. Always give him boils. The general will probably have the boils all day. Hopes you will excuse him. Hopes to see you at tea shop tomorrow."

We decided to go shooting without the general. With four armed bodyguards, two in front and two in the rear, we left the mission around three o'clock in the afternoon, proceeding stealthily up narrow side streets, staying close to shaded walls until we came to the far end of the paved main street. An old man looked up with surprise from his contemplation; he had since followed the sunlight to the opposite side of the street. Passing him, I cocked my .45 and took it off safety but kept it in its holster on my belt. We walked

brusquely in the middle of the street, conscious of the obsti-
nately amused people in the street and the storekeepers running to the front of their stores. We stopped by the bicycle
shop and peeked in; what we saw was a barber shop, with
high stools sitting before broken-edged mirrors hanging by
wire on rusted, bent nails that stuck out farther than the glass.
Shum gasped something in Chinese.

"I'll be a son of a bitch!" I said, amazed.

"Me, too," Shum reflected.

"This *is* the bicycle shop," I said. "It is, isn't it?"

Hastily Shum shrugged. "Yes. Maybe. Maybe not."

"What the hell, maybe, maybe not? It damn well *was*.
What happened?"

Shum said, "Who knows? Maybe wrong shop. Maybe
went out of business; not many bicycles in Hotien."

I said, "Crap."

A barber clipped hair from a bushy-browed man looking spitefully at himself in the mirror.

"Hmm," Shum considered. "Unusual."

The bodyguards stood by, awaiting action.

"Let's go," Shum said. "Unless you want a haircut?"

That evening Shum and I went to the best tea shop to
get drunk. General Wu was there, drinking tea and eating
poppyseed cakes. The front room upstairs hummed with mosquitoes racing around the table, racing around the oil lamp,
racing in to join the group through the canopied front on the
paved street. The street was dark, and occasional triangles of
conversation moved by the shop.

"The old bastard's eating poppyseed cakes," I said. "Tell
him they're bad for his boils."

The general waved us to seats. His eyes hid a secret.

"Tell him, Shum. Dammit."

Shum and General Wu talked and laughed and talked some more.

"General Wu says fine to tell you at this excellent moment," Shum said. "An hour of triumph for the forces of freedom. A superb catastrophe has occurred to the Nip devils." He drank a cup of tea (a small gulp was all the tea a cup held). "Guess what?" he added, grinning.

"Do not know *guess what.*"

"It's this way." Shum leaned back on the stool. "Japs are in bicycle shop. You are not wrong."

"I know that."

"Ah, no. You said you didn't know. You were wrong but you were right. Ha, ha. You know?"

"All right, I don't know."

"Nothing?"

"Not a damn thing. Where the hell am I?"

"Ha, ha, Dan. You don't know. You admit?"

"Ha, ha," I answered. "I don't know. I admit."

"It happens," he said, looking sometimes at the fat general and sometimes at me, "that General Wu hears that Japs send special Japs to kill you. He finds that out from private sources, and relays information to General Tong, who expresses equal concern over your welfare. Both men want to see you alive and successful in your work. They feel they must observe comings and goings of strangers with the highest scrutiny— is that word right?" I nodded that it was, and he went on. "They miss the Japs this morning that see you. You find them, he says. When we go to tea shop and tell General Wu, he immediately gets to talking with General Tong. They send some of their soldiers to the bicycle shop and arrest the spies while they eat lunch. Rice."

"Is that all?" I grinned; it made me feel good to know that I had spotted the Japs. "Why did the bicycle shop turn into a barber shop?"

"Ah. Ha, ha, sometimes commerce moves quickly in China. You don't understand that. Businessmen sell stores like that maybe few times each month. Fast work today."

I asked them why they hadn't let me know of the danger before today.

General Wu rumbled his shoulders and belly and spoke to Shum. "Worry makes you thin," Shum said. "The general says he has probably never worried since he was two years old. He says you are still living."

I admitted that I thought I was; but what could we be sure of in this world of puzzles?

General Wu spoke to Shum. "The sun and the moon on certain days," Shum said, "and when we die, of a grave on the side of a mountain."

Shum also knew of the spies before I did. "Why didn't you tell me this yesterday?" I asked him.

"I didn't want you to worry," he said.

9

TALE OF A TIGER

LUNG FOUND another woman to replace the spy woman named Ha, and in a few weeks he was happy again. Shum renewed an old interest in birds. He said he was full of contentment, and he looked at the sky all day.

Each of us adopted hobbies from time to time to ward off the deadly boredom of reporting weather conditions in a region where there was little change from day to day. The four daily reports to headquarters could have been prepared with a high degree of accuracy two or three days in advance. This is often what I did. Lying on the balcony with one sleepy eye open, I was able to see a clear quarter of the sky: that meant a cloudless report. Raising myself on one elbow, I looked down at the land: light ground fog almost every morning. Then I sat up on the edge of the slat bed, opened both eyes, thrust a hand into the croaker sack full of ashes, and sifted a featherweight mass in my hand; toddling hazily to the balustrade, I leaned over the rough wet cement and opened my hand. The ashes floated gently to the ground; there was no wind, so I wrote zeroes in the spaces for wind direction and wind force. After a twirl of the psychrometer to measure the aqueous vapor in the air, I finished the report, gave it to Lung to send to headquarters, and lay down.

"You spend too much time in sack," Shum said one morning.

"What do you want me to do? Fight Japs?"

"Do anything," he urged. "Study birds."

"I don't like birds," I confided. "Hate 'em, in fact."

"There is a tale of tiger in this area who likes to chew young Americans who stay in sack too much."

"Be forewarned," I said, "of a giant perching bird wearing a pince-nez who eats young Chinese who wakes young Americans."

"Okay!" Shum said.

The next morning he made a similar observation, and when he said okay four times, I decided that we must do something that would interrupt the dull pattern of our days. Towns were divided into two categories, towns with girls in the tea shops and towns with no girls in the tea shops. A couple of neighboring towns had fine girl tea shops. Ho-Po had three girl tea shops, and we had visited that town twice. Ho-Po, it seemed, was next on the docket. The next morning before the first schedule, I got up and dressed in my walking clothes, which differed from my stay-at-mission apparel only by the addition of heavy wool walking stockings and a floppy straw sun hat.

In this garb, I woke Shum, who sat up suddenly and asked his most recently learned English sentence, "What is up?"

"You."

"Not up," he announced with a groan. "Japs do not get up before seven. I either."

"Get up, Shum."

"Is it time now for weather?"

"You and I are going to take a trip. We're going to investigate the sky in other places. Maybe you'll see some new birds."

"Old birds fine. Good night."

"All the old birds have gone to Ho-Po today. We're going to follow them."

"You want quail in girl tea shop town, no doubting." Shum forced a smile.

"All right now, get up. We're going right after breakfast."

"Is Lung up?" Shum asked.

"He's not going. He'll stay here in case an agent returns with important information."

"What, of weather reports?" he asked undismayed, trying to find an out.

I said I would prepare the reports in advance.

Shum shook his head. He seemed to be in counsel with himself, shrugging his head and shoulder on one side and referring to doubtful advice from the other side; a final, resolute shrug forced the indecision from his mind. "Okay," he answered.

The ancient brown village of Ho-Po stood, like Hotien,

on the bank of a river, dignified, proud, and listless with the brownness of centuries. Its river was wide, and from its slow green flow the village crawled in slopes up from the sampans. The decaying backs of stores and residences, forming a medieval tapestry with faded colors, ascended as though their builders had had Gothic aspirations for a stage setting; you felt spires should be seen rising from the town. Past one row of houses was a main street marching parallel to the river. At either end of the street there were high wooden gates that were drawn shut at night to discourage bandits. Maybe this shutting was a tradition. The faded greenness of the landscape beyond the gates reflected the burned-out appearance of bleached cloth, not prophesying much power even at the farthest horizons, where tall mountains shadowed smaller ones and the almost imperceptible border of hills. Out beyond the east gate and a few hundred yards of narrow paddy path was a congregation of palms bowing to a once-whitened mission house, its church, and its school building. The house was a two-story square with porches surrounding it on both floors, giving it the appearance of a ship with a missing prow and stern, and had been the home of an American missionary who had been killed by the Japanese on an unexpected thrust inland early in the war. You could touch the pompons of the trees from the second-story porch. A line of frayed lanterns, attached to a rope, was suspended from the rafters of the porch ceiling. The house had been uninhabited since the death of the missionary, except during our previous excursions to the girl tea shops in town.

As soon as we crossed the river and arrived at the mission house the complexion of the sky began to change: continents of blue that ordinarily appeared among the clouds at that time of day were hidden. The gargoyles of the clouds mushroomed into anvils; beneath them, lighter clouds scudded pennon-like in the wind, and thunder ripped and jigsawed with fierceness. The tips of the mountains were in the mouths of the clouds.

"No fun tonight," Shum said wryly, as we stood on the upper porch. Southward, and up the paddy valley, faraway curtains of rain began opening and closing, advancing to Ho-Po. Rice paddies swelled into lakes and waved in tensive movements. "Never mind," I said. "This is a girl tea shop town, and we're going to get to town after the rain."

We went inside. The furniture was a careless mixture of solid Victorian and utilitarian Chinese of many dynasties. Odors of old age and musk filled the house. Framed in the hall was an invocation to God to bless the house, written on linen in German. Upstairs I spent an hour rummaging in drawers and cabinets; there were some notes in an elegant, archaic handwriting in the form of a diary begun in 1906; many years were missing. In the bottom drawer of a wardrobe I found neatly tied bundles of *Reader's Digest*s containing articles on sex, painless childbirth, and basketball in the Philippine Islands.

Shum came in from the porch. "Soon I hope rain will come," he said. "I know it will."

A dampness was in the air, and outside the green-brown land was luminously glazed by the cloud motions; shortly, curtains of rain began drumming an intricate tattoo on the tin roof of the mission. On the pathways coolies hastened to farm shelters. Then the rain deepened, making a noise of its own; and southward the mountains were within the clouds.

When the rain stopped it was still dark, but the darkness belonged to day. We went to town, trudging through the mud, and found a tea shop that we had not visited before.

A popeyed man with lank hair down over his eyes, like an inscrutable sheepdog, led us up a rickety stairway to a room on the second floor facing the main street.

Shum worked on the order with the waiter, whose eyes expanded as Shum described what he wanted. The waiter shuffled out, and in a few minutes two girls, one lovely, with schoolgirl pigtails, the other a gangly cut-out of a woman, angular and black-haired with bangs awning her forehead almost down to her bovine brown eyes, came in.

The lovely girl contemplated us. I stared at her. Her soft black hair seemed to betray the confidence of her look. She was a small girl, not much over five feet tall and thin as a spring shoot, and as she raised her arm to arrange a wisp of hair fallen over an ear, her white silk blouse became taut and, like her shadow stretching fractionally on the paper wall, revealed small, firm breasts.

As though they were pursuing a part in a play, the two girls smiled simultaneously. I looked at a couple of stools around the table, smiled at the stools, then at the lovely girl. The thin one went to Shum and sat down awkwardly on his lap. Shum flopped his arms oafishly across her shoulders.

My girl put her wine cup down and with expert care fed me melon seeds. She smiled faintly, not greatly overcharged by the presence of my roving hand.

"Mine is beautiful," I said. "Too bad about yours."

"Okay," Shum said.

"Okay, hell. Where's her superstructure?"

"Do not know *superstructure*," he said.

"All around here," I said, demonstrating on my girl.

Shum nodded. "Ho," he remarked pleasantly. He pressed his girl's hips. "My girl is bone," he said, sighing.

He called the waiter. "Foggy loy!"

The waiter returned with food: rice buried under five different preparations, four of vegetable and one that had a distinct cast of gravel. The girls didn't eat. They fed us and smiled, cooled the air with straw fans, and served as a mosquito-warning team; they smiled and smiled, and grinned when I blocked a chopstickful of unsightly and distasteful food.

"I'd rather eat the girls than this crap," I said.

"Not eat my girl. All bone," Shum said. "Miss Bones."

The waiter approached and spoke to Shum.

"Waiter says we must not play with girls in tea shop," Shum said. "Stay here?"

"We could sit here all night and all we'd get would be sprained hands," I said. "Let's go to the mission."

Shum queried the waiter, who answered with either one or two raised eyebrows. The girls were not interested in the transactions with the waiter; they were both singing in broken squeals higher than the right end of a piano. I said, "This sure is a crock. You sound like hell." They didn't stop; rather, they raised their voices even higher. I put my hand over the mouth of my girl. She put out her tongue. The other girl laughed and went on with her squealing. I tickled them; they weren't ticklish.

"Shum," I interrupted. "Shum, how do you turn them off?"

He looked disinterested. "No way," he said. "They are singing about you. They say you are playboy all around the world."

The popeyed man relaxed behind Shum.

"We must go other place," Shum said. He drank his wine, glanced back over his shoulder, and continued. "It is not nice for us to play with girls here. He say we can go other place if girls want it, but in here playing with girls give tea shop bad name." Shum laughed. "Owner says they are here to serve tea and keep sweetness in the air."

"Ask my girl if she'd like to come out to the mission and have a party now."

"She says she likes parties."

"I want to know if she want to go now."

"She says yes, will come. Likes you."

"Tell her I think she's lovely and the hottest thing this side of Choir Road. Tell her she keeps sweetness in the air."

"She says she will have much pleasure, she hopes."

"Tell her to shut up."

I put my hand hard over her mouth. "What's your name, you lovely squealing bitch?"

She smiled, kissed my ear, and whistled in it.

"I think I'll call you Sing Hi," I said. "Your voice stinks."

She kissed me again, same place.

"Your confederate's name is Sing Lo. You keep sweetness in the air."

Sing Hi sat on my lap, small and smiling and cracking melon seeds between her very white teeth. Each time she put one in my mouth she kissed me. She was very light, her toes barely touching the floor. I was having a fine time running my hands over her soft and flexible body, clean and incense-smelling and just bronzed like shade on a golden object. "I'd love to sleep with her," I said. "She's very lovely."

"You love her body," Shum said.

"That's right."

"You have luck," Shum said, pinching his girl. "God damn for this girl. Have hard time to pinch her."

"Too thin."

"You say it. Too thin."

I laughed.

"What you have in your mind?" Shum asked.

"Does she sleep with everybody?"

Sing Hi made an O of her mouth and put her hands sorrowfully to her small breasts. Then she smiled.

"'Not on her life,' she says. She must say 'No, no, no' to many guests," Shum said. "She learns to preserve virtue so she can go to heaven. She learns about heaven in mission school and thinks she wants to go to most desirable place."

"Of course."

"You want to sleep with her. She knows you are hero by knowledge of guerrilla fighting with General Tong. She says sleep is good and she likes you. You are playboy of the Western world. That's one word, *siji-ah*, you hear the sound?"

"Yes," I said.

Sing Hi turned around on my lap, trying to block the conversation.

"Does she want to come to the mission now?" I asked.

"Oh, yes," Shum said. "You know that."

Shum called the waiter. They argued about the bill. "Damnation!" Shum bawled. "This bastard puts down here that we owe him for taking two girls from working. He says we must pay a large sum for the sweetness and light if we take them to mission. Damnation!"

Shum threw a wad of bills on the table and we left. The waiter bowed and smiled at the floor in the doorway.

Sing Hi, even on the narrow viaduct of mud through the rice paddies, managed to walk gracefully. Shum walked with the exaggeratedly straight posture of a drunkard. His girl mimicked him. On a particularly treacherous turn Shum slid off into a paddy, and, landing in a submerged and almost horizontal position, he made no attempt to get up but looked evenly in our direction. Sing Lo decided to help him. She took off her sandals, rolled up her black silk trousers to her bony knees, and skied off the embankment onto his lap. She started to sing.

Sing Hi and I left them and went on carefully to the mission. We lit the kerosene lamp on the table by the stairway and went to the front bedroom on the porch. While she washed her feet in a pan of water, I went outside with a handful of candles and lit them in the lanterns.

She muttered something I could not understand, and I called back, "I'll bet you're pretty. Wait there."

Inside, I blew out the flame of the lamp by the bed, and a moment later paper lantern light, damask and solferino beacons, traveled into the room and through our mosquito netting and dispatched, returning the pattern of the bed's brassworks into gray-black crenellations on the wall. A gentle wind intermittently billowed the netting in on one side and out of the other.

Sing Hi was small and warm and soft, and she seemed to anticipate every emotion. She sang a Chinese song that sounded like a child's lullaby. But it wasn't a lullaby, despite the melody. The words were foul, and I had heard them before. When she stopped, she clapped her hands without noise and kissed me.

"You sweet bitch!" I said, pulling her nearer. "Who would think you knew such songs." I started to sing the song in Chinese. Sing Hi pulled away and played see no evil, speak no evil, hear no evil with her hands and then repeated the same on me.

I caught one of her two short braided pigtails and slipped off the rubber bands that held it. Her hair flushed like a dark waterfall down one side of her face, hiding one eye, like Veronica Lake. "Christmas! You look funny!" I tried to undo the other pigtail, but Sing Hi held it firmly behind her ear. She squealed a song I did not know and then she laughed slowly. I didn't know what she was laughing at, but I supposed that she expected me to laugh with her.

She pulled the sheet over her head and repeated, "Christmas! You look funny!"

"You look funny," I said, and told her, in Chinese, that the phrase meant I loved her. I could also tell somebody to go to hell in Chinese; basic words, concerning the enemy and daily needs, formed my vocabulary.

"I love you, *b'd'ung?*" I said.

"I love you, *b'd'ung?*" Sing Hi repeated in the same tone. She came out of the sheet, smiling securely.

Sing Hi stopped smiling and said, "Honestry?"

I gasped.

"What did you say?" I asked, bewildered by the sound of English.

"You love me, honestry?"

Instead of answering her question, I asked her where the hell she had learned to speak English.

She looked very serious, not as though she had planned to surprise me.

"I wish to say in tea shop," she said, "but you make many bad words, I not sure you speak English."

I repeated my question, wondering if I shouldn't forget that Sing Hi had spoken English. I mean, God, I was all mixed up; it's quite a serious matter to tell someone you love her when she understands you.

She came closer. "In mission school I have best grade: A.

Very good student. Learn much English. To heart's content. I finish school and go work for English family in Swatow before Japanese come. Then come back to Ho-Po."

"And play a joke on me," I said bitterly.

"Ha, ha, you never think I am English lady. You think I squealing bitch!"

"No."

"You say."

"I didn't mean that," I begged. "That was a figure of speech."

She shook her head. "You speech bad," she said. "In mission school we learn to speech nicely. To heart's content."

"Honestry?" I asked.

"You very mean."

Christ! I felt mean. As soon as the thought that she was a tea shop girl ran through my mind, it was followed by the observation that this girl was lovely and gentle and could smile at me with intelligent and independent brown eyes, and she was lovely in bed and had given herself to me and I had loved her for a moment.

"You're very wrong," I said. "I thought you were a Chinese lady. You're lovely."

"Ha, ha, I squealing bitch!" she said huskily. "What my name? You call me Sing Hi."

"That's because I didn't know your name. Nobody introduced us. You came into our room at the tea shop and sat on my lap. What should I call you?"

She looked at me from the corners of her eyes. "Little girls who go to mission have Christian names. Anna. Elizabeth. Dorothy. Amy. My name is—you guess."

I guessed Dorothy.

She laughed. "I are Amy."

"Amy Hi?"

"Amy. No Hi. You make up Hi. You very mean."

"Now, Amy," I said, and somehow my feelings of callousness disappeared when I said her name, "I was a big dope. I didn't mean to say those things. They weren't nice. I'm sorry."

"Dope," she said, "dope. What is dope? Dope, dope, dope."

"Foolish man," I explained. "Not a playboy. Not mean. Just foolish. You know fool?"

"Hmmm. Yes. Yes. Fool. You big fool."

"I was just that," I said. "You are Amy and I are a big dope. I will be nice."

"You will be nice," she said.

Abruptly she turned her head, revealing the quiet line of a thin, arching eyebrow and the adamant fullness of her cheek held in the cup of her hand. Her lips came hard together, and then she moved urgently. A narrow corridor of wind swung the lanterns one after another, and abstract meetings of lights pendulumed over us and through the netting, the lights rising and falling and fading out.

When our bodies were complete and no longer anxious, we clung to each other for a very long time.

"If I knew another language," I said, softly, "I'd call you a lovely witch. I love you. Savvy?"

"You love me?"

"Yes, I do. You come back to Hotien with me. We'll make a big housekeeping in Hotien."

"What I do when you go from Hotien?"

"I won't be going for many months."

"When war is over, Amy is over. You go home. No more Sing Hi. I have to stay alone. To my heart's content."

"Maybe I'll stay in Hotien." It seemed an easy thing to lie. "Maybe we'll go to America." I didn't want to lie, but I did. I wanted her to come to Hotien.

Amy sat up in bed against the pillow. She didn't speak, and in a moment she came back into bed and put her arms around me. "You talking too much," she said. "My missionary teacher says Americans honor all Commandments."

Her obstinate intelligence made me insistent. She could come to Hotien and I could find her a room in town.

"Amy, Amy, Amy," I whispered in the kisses. "You come to Hotien."

"Squealing bitch," she said. "No savvy."

"*Mama foo-foo*," I said. The words meant "never mind" and "not very good" and a thousand other things.

In the morning I got up early and went outside on the porch. Light strained through layers of clouds, high and firm, and beyond the town small gray-white clouds gathered in cumulus fleets in the harbors of the mountain range, now washed and cleansed with long purple sea shadows. There was a slight wind.

I went back inside, careful not to wake Amy, and rummaged through some of the old magazines and the scattered pages from the missionary's diary. The missionary, I discovered, had come to China from a Bible college in Ohio at the beginning of the century. With humble humor he mentioned their trials in the first years: recurrent demands and diplomacies extended at risk to roaming warlords and bandit generals; Chinese antiques (an insufficient word, he claimed, to describe centuries-old pieces of brass and silver and silken tapestries) hunted down through research and letter writing to all the provinces. He wrote with pride of the construction and dedication of the mission's church and school, of the converts to his religion and the first marriages in the new church, of an incident that illustrated the difficulty of teaching Christianity to the Chinese: on his walks through the rice paddies he would hear coolies observe after him, "There goes Jesus Christ." His advice to a new missionary was "Keep sweet or else go home."

I put the diary on the table and tried to feel some of the missionary's experiences. The sky had focused into a blue and white checkerboard sifting cautiously lower to earth. In a gallery of clouds I studied shapes and faces. Amy woke up and moved in the bed; she rested her head against my shoulder. "You do not love me," she said in a sleepy voice. Nuts! The face in the cloud gallery was Hernando Cortez discovering an altar of religious gold in Mexico. An incision of blue opened for an eye. It glared at another cloud-face for a moment, winked, and disappeared, closing into whiteness. Suddenly the portraits blended into a kaleidoscope of blue and white columns as if the wind had parted the world. What the hell did Amy have to gab about love for? For what? They got hold of a couple of English words and ran them into the ground. She probably meant something different from Webster anyway. Hell, she was lovely and I would love to have her in Hotien, but I sure as hell didn't love her. "Lovely girl," I said. Amy said something I didn't understand and put her arms around my neck. It didn't make a goddam bit of difference, I decided, whether she could speak English or whether she was mute.

Shum and his girl were seated at the refectory table in the kitchen eating rice when we came downstairs. They were eating out of blue bowls, and in the middle of the table was a plain blue pitcher holding a bunch of yellow flowers with too-long stems. The sun's rays cut into the room, quickly lighting the table. There was a fat cook shuffling in front of the stove. I had no idea where she had come from. She looked up and smiled at Amy and me. "Ding hao! Ho, ho, ho!" she said.

Amy and I sat down. The girls giggled at each other; they seemed extremely self-possessed. Shum's girl was awfully ugly in daylight. I couldn't imagine her at the mission school. I smiled at her and she grinned.

The food was very good, the rice was covered with some new vegetables, and we shared a cucumber that had grown in the garden in the back yard. We drank a bottle of lousy rice wine; Shum said the wine had been bought in Kityang, down the river, where the Japs had a garrison.

"God," Shum complained, "bony girl. Not even one good pinch. Nothing. Bones."

I wanted to tell Shum that Amy spoke English, but he went on before I could say it.

"In bed, in dark, maybe all right," he admitted, rubbing his chin. "But, griefs, can't stand to look at her. You have nice girl. Soft baby. Very pretty."

"Thank you. That's true. She's very lovely."

Amy drank another cup of wine, glancing at me above the rim of her cup. She nodded.

"We go back?" Shum asked.

"No go back," I said.

"Tomorrow?"

"Okay."

"Good," Shum said. "I like it here. I like the bony girl. Maybe you like her. I let you have her tonight."

"No thanks."

Amy got up to get some more rice from the stove.

"Shum, you think maybe I can take her back to Hotien?"

Amy turned around, watching Shum. Her hair was

parted, without pigtails, so that most of it brushed to one side. She looked older without the pigtails.

"That's all right," he said. "Really all right."

"The shinfoo would bless it, wouldn't he?"

"Yes. He say okay."

"I'm sure of it," I said, knowing that Father Tan would be most unhappy. "She could live in town. Not come to the mission."

"Oh, wonderful idea," Shum said, amused. "You have woman in Hotien and the shinfoo makes us leave his mission."

"Ask Sing Hi if she'd come back with me."

"She says you only joking."

"No, I'm not," I said.

Amy and I looked at each other while Shum spoke.

"She asks do you have love for her?"

"Sure."

"She says you speak very bad of her at tea shop."

"Tell her I'm sorry."

They spoke to each other; Amy looked contritely at me over her shoulder. What the hell's wrong with her, I thought.

Shum smiled like a dishonest judge as he said, "Sweety says she loves you, thinks you are lovely boy, but won't come to Hotien." Then he moaned. "Ah, the bony girl. She come if you want. What luck."

Amy came back to the table, looking sad. Hell, she was lovely, and I didn't come to Ho-Po to get married. I leaned over and whispered in her ear. She moved her chair nearer and began to eat rice from my bowl.

Shum grinned. "You have good time, I see."

"Yes," I answered.

"Why you don't feel good?"

"I feel fine," I said. "What makes you think I don't?"

"You say too much bad language."

"What the hell, Shum? I'm having a fine time."

"Hope you calm down language," he said.

"Fine. Fine," I said. "I believe I shall."

"When we go back?" he asked.

"Tomorrow. Maybe next day. Maybe next week. Maybe stay here."

"Not good to do. Rain is not in report. It looks like rain."

"It always looks like rain," I said. "That's why we came here. To check on the rain. You take it easy."

"Hell."

Amy whispered in my ear, "You no tell Shum I speak English."

"What she say?" Shum asked.

"She told me the bony girl loves you with all her heart and knows that you are her best friend in the world."

"Damn lie," Shum said.

"No, it's the damn truth. Look at the loving smile on her face as she looks at you."

Shum looked and sighed. "Oh, damn," he said.

"Maybe you want to take her to Hoticn," I suggested.

Shum groaned. "You crazy," he said.

Sing Lo hadn't stopped eating for fifteen minutes; that's a lot of rice.

Shum grabbed Sing Lo and they stood up. "I think I go to town and look for things," he said. "Perhaps another girl. We see you at tea shop for supper. Okay?"

"All right," I said. "Don't get lost."

Shum pulled her out of the kitchen.

I took Amy's hand and her body was excited. We kissed,

and after the kisses we dumped the rice back in the pot on the stove. "Ding hao! Ding hao!" the old cook wailed as we left. "Ho, ho, ho!"

"Ho, ho to you grandmother," I replied. *"Ding hao* yourself."

After we had been in bed a few hours, Amy spoke some submerged half-forgotten English and I got serious and remembered what she had said during the night. She pronounced my name "Tan," and though I told her to say "Dan," she somehow couldn't pronounce it correctly. It seemed awfully easy lying in bed, watching the afternoon clouds coming low and fast and dark, to imagine myself really in love with her. And I talked about love. About her coming to Hotien.

"You have me in Hotien, and when you go, I stay alone," Amy said. "No fun for me when you go. I remembers you and am sad whole life."

I said we were in a war and we couldn't be sure of what would happen after it was over.

"Oh," she exclaimed, "you are like stupid Chinese soldier. They say same in tea shop."

I was flustered. "You don't understand," I said.

"You say love, love, love. What you mean love? You mean I come with you for sleeping."

"You don't mean love, love, love when you work in tea shops," I said. I couldn't help saying the wrong thing; I wanted out, but I wanted her.

Later, Amy said, "I love you, but I no go." She kissed me. "In Swatow I work for English family and they introduce young English boy who says he loves Amy and will take Amy with him if the Japanese come to get the city. But they come and he not take me. I love him and he tells not the truth."

"I wouldn't do that," I said. Hell! So that's how she learned English! I almost said that aloud.

"No," she said flatly. "You come to sleep with tea shop girl. No love."

I mean, what the hell! How senseless could you get, arguing about love with a tea shop girl? The devil with it.

I got dressed and went downstairs, waiting for her to come. It was late, the sky was purple and hazy, and we had to hurry to meet Sing Lo and Shum. We left the mission as soon as she came down, without saying a word.

The tea shop was not crowded. A party was going on loudly in the front room; we could hear them in the street. The fat smells rolled from the kitchen, and a bald old man with young, inquisitive eyes sat outside inhaling his special ribbon of odor. Three men stood in front idly talking. Amy said she had to talk to the popeyed man; she went upstairs. In a minute Shum came down. I got into conversation with the old man; that is, we both talked and waited for the other to answer, but we didn't understand each other.

"Sing Hi speaks English," I said to Shum, turning my back to the old man.

"Ha, ha," Shum laughed. "She understands you."

"That's what I said."

"You want her to come to Hotien?"

"Yes," I said. "But she doesn't want to come."

"She's, ah," Shum's voice became pontifical, "very lovely girl. She has many, how you say? friends." Shum added another thought: "How's her English? Good like me?"

"Oh, no, Shum, nobody's English can beat yours," I said. "She says 'honestry' and 'to my heart's content.' She worked in Swatow before the Japs came."

"Oh, I see," he said.

Amy and the bony girl came outside, and we walked on down the main street. The stores were slatted up except for a few food shops. The heat of the evening settled in the street like a fog cloud, but off the main street toward the river we saw the tops of trees moving and we went to the river bank to find the wind.

The alleyway we passed through was high and windowless and smelled of burning dung and lime. When we came into the open Shum took his fingers away from his nose and breathed the clean air. The water was brown around the sampans but clear and silver-gray farther out. Here and there a sampan family appeared in the dim, sticky light of their oil lamp, squatting on the stern around a brazier. Near us a family chomped rice from a black pot on the fire. The children looked like weak birds sheltered in delicate nests; and as we watched them, Amy put her hand in mine. I said nothing but watched the sampan family intently. The father put his chopsticks on the deck in a jar of water. He got up and went to the bow which was away from us, and sat down over the side and relieved himself. He came back to the fire and took his chopsticks. No one seemed to say anything, the mother hadn't even looked up during the man's absence, and the children didn't need urging to finish their supper. Shum and Sing Lo moved away from us, up the bank. "Real Hakka boat," Amy said. "Very sad life. Bad luck for women to come on Hakka boats. Old superstition."

"What about his wife?" I said.

"Bad luck for him," she said.

The sampan family finished eating and went under the matting roof. Flickers of light dotted the straw, and on the neighboring boats other families had finished eating and began washing their faces and arms with the river water. I felt strangely uncomfortable, aware of the poverty and misery, relayed from unknown and relentless sources, that made Amy work in a tea shop and the sampan family live on an unclean boat. It made me feel, perhaps, a sympathy and a pity for everyone around me. I felt pity for her and I hated that feeling. I was certain that pity merely helped to assuage my own feelings of defeat at not getting her to come back with me. And then the feeling changed: hell! she probably had the same opinion of me that I'd heard the Chinese women had of Americans in Kunming. I was an American, like all the rest, with big somethings and blue eyes. Nuts! But Amy didn't have any feelings on her face.

The night came and the river was clean and the trees waved tiredly and there was no noise but the gentle wooden rubbing of the sampans.

The stone bridge at the end of town was occasionally lighted by a late traveler coming into town or by a farmer returning to his home in the country. A fresh green smell wafted in from across the river, and now in the night the water seemed to be moving faster and washing away the impurities of the day's living. Slight phosphorescent glows tinged the current. It was a different river now, and many fish might be running down to the sea, to the cauldron of life, and the town to them was maybe the dim lights on the sampans and the deeper shadows under the big stone bridge. In another few days they would swim to the ocean. I wondered what their life would be like without the boundaries of narrow banks and a shallow bottom. Well, that was something for the fish to decide. I had my own troubles.

Amy and I walked down to the bridge on the plank wharf. Under the bridge we kissed many times and said nothing.

Rain fell suddenly. A light rain. One of the gentle rains that makes things grow. The lights on the sampans began to go out. We stood for a while under the bridge, dry and sheltered except for the overreaching drizzles that slanted in on us. Then we went back to the main street through the empty alleyway.

Shum and the bony girl stood inside the tea shop, waiting for us. We went upstairs; the popeyed man served us in the front room. The town was quiet, and the popeyed man looked sleepy. He dropped his habit of hurrying and smiling. After he brought in a tray of tea and rice cakes, he leaned against the wall and spoke excitedly to Shum for a few minutes.

"He wants us to pay him for sweetness and light," Shum said with a smile. "Miss Bones, I think, worth no pay. Miss Sing Hi, you pay for her one million dollars CN."

"That's right," I said.

"I tells him money we pay is for her. Not Old Bones," Shum said, saluting Amy.

Shum paid the popeyed man. He didn't seem glad to have the money.

"What's his trouble, Shum?"

"Oh, he thinks we make him work too hard. No girls to work in tea shop."

As we got up to leave, I asked Shum to tell the man to give some of that money to Amy and his other girl.

"He wants girls working tomorrow," Shum said.

"Tell him to go to hell."

"What shall I say?" Shum asked.

"We'll leave in the morning," I said.

"He says he wants girls now."

"Tell him to shove off."

"I better speak to him," Shum said, handing the popeyed man another wad of money. "I tell him we leave early."

That night at the mission we sat up drinking rice wine outside on the porch, laughing and cursing. Once in the early morning we heard rolling echoes of gunfire. Foraging Japs in a hill town were celebrating something. Mosquitoes attacked and we went to our beds where the netting protected us. Shum followed Sing Lo to their room, calling, "Cheerio!"

"She'd look wonderful in Hotien," I said.

Amy and I got into bed without talking. She fell asleep immediately. I tried to think about her, but things were hazy and I too was asleep soon.

I got up before the sun and kissed Amy after I had dressed. She moved slightly, still sleeping. Then I tickled her nose with a pigtail and she sat up with an "Ai-yah!"

"Time to get up," I said. "Train leaving for Hotien in half a century."

"You go on train?"

"Yes. Special car."

"Special train for Amy?"

"Yes. Same car."

She sat up in bed, naked.

"I sad already," she said. "I remember you to my heart's content."

"You don't have to be sad," I said. "Come to Hotien."

"Then I am more sad."

I lay down again, and when Amy got up first to get dressed, I thought she might come with me, but when I became serious downstairs and she suddenly laughed and said, "Sing Hi squealing bitch! Squealing bitch!" I knew she wouldn't come.

Shum was happy at breakfast. "Miss Bones I see not after today. Hot dog!"

The bony girl turned her head lackadaisically on a sullen and disinterested axis. Shum's manner of referring to her seemed to deprive her of any individuality. Incurious, she was just a horse-faced tea shop girl, neither pleasant nor unpleasant, and not especially solicitous.

We got ready to go. The fat old cook puttered about, closing up the mission, and she waved as we left the yard.

I kissed Amy in front of the tea shop, and two grinning loungers laughed in the cloth shop next door; then Shum and I quickly left the main street and walked on the plank wharf to the bridge. We followed the river path across the bridge, turning left. We had gone not more than a few hundred yards when we began meeting farmers coming to town with produce in huge straw baskets on yoke sticks across their shoulders, balancing them like giant scales.

A heavily-muscled farmer wearing wide-seated trousers approached with a band of dogs. Coming closer, I noticed that the dogs had rope strings around their necks and the strings were attached to a bamboo pole.

"What the hell?" I wondered aloud.

"Dogs go to food shop," Shum answered.

That rather made me sick. I bent down to pat a mangy black dog struggling hopefully on the edge of the path. The dog bared carious teeth and growled.

"Looks like my girl," Shum said.

The path turned from the river and up a hill. We looked back from the hillside, glanced across the low paddy land to Ho-Po awaking in a morning mist, then hurried on.

We reached Hotien in time to change the twelve-thirty weather report to include the clouds. As soon as he finished the transmission, Lung wanted to know everything about the trip. He didn't believe what I told him. "Big lie," he said. "Lie or dream. Why she not here?"

"She didn't want to leave," I answered.

"Strange," Lung said.

I began to worry during the week. There was something I almost felt and understood.

"You love tea shop girl," Lung said one afternoon. "Why you no marry? Chinese marriage. I do."

The shinfoo's unhappy black mongrel came up to us in the garden. Lung bent down, caught hold of him, and scratched him behind his ears. "Bring girl here," he said. "Chinese marriage. All right for me, all right for you," he said. "Okay for Father Tan. Good for him."

Lung's thick eyebrows lowered toward the bridge of his nose, and he looked critically at the balcony where Father Tan was standing. Lung waved to him.

The shinfoo waved back.

"She doesn't want to come here," I said.

"You wrong, I know," Lung said.

"No, I'm not."

"I know," he said. "You go there. She comes to Hotien. She comes with you."

Then, late in the evening, while I was at the radio listening to some popular music from Shanghai, I suddenly thought of her and had to go to Ho-Po. No one ever took a long trip at night on the paths of China. I had been told that a long time ago. But I started out alone and walked maybe halfway there when I got suddenly tired and could go no farther. I lay down on a hillock off the path, in the dampness, but I fell asleep and didn't wake until late in the morning. There was a stream near the path and I went to it and took off my clothes. I stayed in the stream swimming and splashing in the cool water until after a while I felt a warm current against my legs and, looking upstream, saw a hundred feet away, partly hidden by outstretched maples, three water buffaloes. They stood in the water up to their stomachs, and when they saw me watching them, they snorted and their backs heaved. A farmer was standing on the bank. I yelled at him, although I didn't expect him to understand me. I yelled at him to take his goddam animals out of the water. I wanted to swim in clean water.

The farmer saw me. He waved a couple of times and watched the water buffaloes.

I got out and dried myself on the bank. Then I got dressed and started walking. I passed the farmer and threatened him again. He laughed and pointed to his water buffaloes and grabbed himself below. The water buffaloes turned sideways downstream and looked pitifully at me.

I walked upward in the cool, green hills and then down again in the humid valley lands near the village. It was midday when I got to the tea shop. Thunderheads were ballooning in the sky, shadows covered the stalls in the main street, and idlers standing in doorways were part of movements frozen in the shade. At the tea shop the popeyed man looked surprised when he saw me. He began to bow but I stopped him. I pointed up the stairway and then in the direction of the mission. He bowed. He smiled without expression and went upstairs.

The smell of food cooking in oils in iron bowls seeped in the clean shade of the room off the pavement. A few Chinese stood in there, waiting for me to smile so that they could smile too.

The man returned, stood stiffly in front of me, and bowed. Rising, he shook his head and spoke in Chinese. I didn't understand. *"B'd'ung,"* I said, "I don't understand."

He pantomimed sleep, putting his clasped hands to his ear and slanting his head. I tore off a piece of wrapping paper on the counter and wrote a note to her. I handed it to the popeyed man and pointed again.

The Chinese looked anxiously at me. They wanted to smile. The man shook his head and went upstairs.

He returned in a few minutes and put a piece of paper in my hand. The same note I had given him. Below my message Amy had written: "No savez?" The Chinese stared hard. They knew they were going to get a chance to smile. I rolled the paper into a bullet and threw it hard at one of the bastards. A couple of them looked at each other and laughed softly.

10

A HOUSE ON

HIECHECHIN BAY

AT 7:30 IN the morning one day early in July, we received a message which Shum and I began decoding; I looked up the encoded letters on the permanent cross-section alphabet on the back of our one-time pad, found the new letters, and called them off for him to write down.

"Say, look at this," said Shum, just as I was falling into a fast rhythm. "We have no message like this before." He was unusually excited. "I wonder what is up."

"What is it, the old guy telling us not to get captured?"

"No. He doesn't say that." Shum looked puzzled.

"Good news?" I asked.

He said, "I hope," and handed me the message.

I read the form:

PUNCH FROMF LETCH ERXTH ISTOP SECRE TINFO RMATI
ONFOR YOURP ERUSA LONLY XUNDE RNOCI RCUMS TANCE
SDIVU LGETH ISINF ORMAT IONTO INTER PRETE RORRA DIOOP
ERATO RX

This became

PUNCH FROM FLETCHER. THIS IS TOP SECRET INFORMATION
FOR YOUR PERUSAL ONLY. UNDER NO CIRCUMSTANCES
DIVULGE THIS INFORMATION TO INTERPRETER OR RADIO
OPERATOR.

Shum looked intently at different objects in the radio room
while I watched and tried to think clearly about the order.

"Maybe I go downstairs. See what Lung is doing."

I told him the hell with that.

"Major Fletcher gets mad. Maybe bad for war effort if I
know message. Might tell it to nearest Japs."

I told him to help decode.

I studied the letters chopped off in blocks of five. "Shum,
see if anyone's outside the door, please."

He got up, went to the door, looked, and came back. "I
see no one," he said.

"Shum, this is really secret, and it's good news. Don't
shout when I tell you what it is."

I asked him whether he knew the bay at Lukfeng. Yes,
certainly, he said, it was on our map, a very long, wide horse-
shoe bay. Water from the Pacific Ocean rested in the bay;
but it wasn't used as a port, either in the past by Chinese ships
or now by the Japs, who anchored instead at Swabue, farther
south, and Hong Kong and north at Swatow.

"The Allies are going to land there," I said.

Shum hit the table with his fist. "I say nothing," he said,

looking as happy as the generalissimo in some of his old pictures.

"This message says between the nineteenth and twenty-ninth of this month. We'll be the nearest station to the landing forces. When they land we'll go to Lukfeng to meet them, providing the Japs don't come after us. If they do, we'll go to the hills and out to sea as fast as we can and we'll say howdy to the admiral and general as they wade ashore. And we'll offer them closest cooperation. They'll get mad—they'll all be mad—when they find that we were here all the time; we're the local reception committee."

"They'll get mad!"

"Yes. Then we'll go aboard a fine ship and stay on it until we reach America. "

"I know," Shum said, "we put a bar of soap in our armpits, that causes fever. I remember medical tricks."

"And we'll get you into medical school there."

"And American citizenship."

"That too. Smuggle you in as honored guest of the fleet. You'll be given twenty-five medals and steak and ice cream three times a day."

"Ah, no," Shum moaned. "I bet first meal is rice with string beans." He hit the table again.

We got a bottle of wine from the small wall cabinet and uncorked it. It lasted many toasts. Shum wiped his mouth with his arm to brush away a wine moustache. "So good," he said.

"Another bottle," I said.

Shum burst into a rolling Chinese song, which he repeated again and again. The melody was nice, the words were dirty and not so nice. He finished with a cheer. "They cannot win war without our station," he said. "This landing cannot happen without our intelligence. We will be great, and future children will read about us in their textbooks."

"Bull, chicken, horse, bat, and owl," I said.

"Yes," he said. "They cannot land without us. What we do now? We sent headquarters maps of the Jap placements all around us and on the coast." He answered himself. "Sit and wait, then run for the Navy."

I nodded. "Yes, and we'll get further instructions, I suppose."

"If major say come back to headquarters," Shum said, "we won't go. Throw the radio away, run for the Navy, say we didn't hear."

"Okay."

We got four bottles of wine and went outside the compound to a shady hillside off the Ho-Po path. We sat down and started drinking the wine. The sun attacked from over a lion-brown ridge stuck with lonely pines whose shadows held a line below the ridge. Pretty soon we got drunk; after we had successfully completed the invasion, had been greeted, medaled, and praised, we dozed off, the sun getting stronger and drying early morning out of the air. And then we fell asleep.

"I say, I say," came a high, strange voice out of my sleep, "you gentlemen display a degree of moral turpitude far above that of any Americans I have seen in China."

I sat up. A tall, skinny white man dressed in baggy black Chinese clothes with a thin, hooked jib of a nose was walking back and forth on the path, four steps this way, four steps that.

Shum woke with a start. "Jesus Christ," he said.

"Amen," the man said.

Shum turned to me. "What the hell?" he asked.

The stranger strode ominously between the two of us. "By swearing and lying and killing and stealing and committing adultery they break out, and blood toucheth blood. Hosea 4:2," he said.

"I think this bastard is preacher," Shum said.

The stranger's hand went up and from the hand there telescoped a finger pointing to a clear blue sky. "I am merely one of a number of the children of God hoping for success as an agent of the United States Navy."

I looked at the guy's Chinese clothes. The Navy had a stupid rule which said that its men behind the lines must wear Chinese clothes to avoid detection. It was a rule I had heard about, sometimes from Navy men, but this was the first time I had seen a walking American wearing a complete Chinese suit.

With him was a young Chinese man, probably no older than Shum, smiling at the man as he spoke. I guessed he was the stranger's interpreter. He had a wide jaw and a narrow forehead, and he wore thin-framed tortoise-shell glasses.

"We don't have Japs here," I said. "Is there anything we can do for you?"

He looked patronizingly at us. "Have you not heard the good word?"

"No," I said. "What good word?"

"The word of God!" he thundered.

I turned to Shum. "The son of a bitch is a preacher," I said.

"My name," he said, "is Hobart Bow. Bow rhymes with cow. Have you heard it before? Never, I'm sure."

A preacher—or a lunatic.

An arm flipped to the boy with glasses. "This sterling future of China I present, Dewey Lum."

Dewey Lum saluted me. "Glorious, lovely day, do you find it not?"

"Bastard!" Shum suddenly shouted. "I know Dewey Lum. We attend same school in Hong Kong. King's College!" They hit each other joyfully.

Dewey Lum and I shook hands.

"Celebration. This is celebration," said Shum, picking up a bottle of wine. He popped it and offered it to his old friend. Shum took a drink and handed the bottle to me, and I gave it to Hobart Bow. He looked at it for a moment, brought it up to his mouth, and finished the bottle. His thick, sandy hair had fallen to near his eyebrows, and he smiled sheepishly and said in a mournful voice, "I have sinned."

"Sit down," I comforted. "Give me the other bottle, Shum."

Bow sat down in the shade and moaned. "I have sinned. I have sinned. I have backslid in China," he said.

"Easy there, fellow," I said. "Can't be that bad."

"It is. It is," he said, holding his hands to stop trembling. "Oh, it's almighty bad. All the good work and now it's gone —to pot."

"What good work?" I said. "Aren't you in the Navy?"

"Ah yes, but that's not the good work I mean. I mean the work which is approved above under the watchful eye of the Lord." He pointed to the blue sky.

"Have another drink," I said.

He turned his face away. His hands were tense, as though he were praying, and he reluctantly waved the bottle away.

He faced us then with a look of resignation and went on, "The work I refer to is that of the missionary of God, that these people may, by the glorious and simple act of faith, enter into the world of the Lord for ever and ever."

"You should wear a hat," Shum said.

I told Shum to shut up and asked Bow to tell us his story.

"I am like that pedestrian benefactor of civilization, the cop," he said, "directing the ways to the lost and the foundering." He dropped his hand, seized the bottle, and took a long drink.

Then Dewey took a long drink and said, pointing to Bow, "He's a Seventh Day Adventist."

Bow struck a pose. "Navy of coursh reshponsible my being in China," he said, "an' f'r ord'rin me this shection." He hiccuped and burped. "But Navy in which I humbly serve as officer although you see no rank on me is not reshponsible my religioush activity. To date have conferted—converted —almost 250 goddam Chinese thish true faith. An' haven't used medishine or shoc'late bars. Either."

Dewey took another long drink. "He tells the truth," he said. "And how!"

Shum took a drink. "Hobart Bow Wow!" he yelled.

I told him to shut up.

"Hobart Bow Wow!" he said.

Bow looked deprecatingly at Shum. Then he took another bottle and started drinking.

"Brother," Dewey Lum said. "Brother! The Navy do not approve, so Mister Bow never tells his commanding officers about the Seven Day religion. He do not tells them about converts."

I took a drink.

"Hobart Bow Wow!" said Shum.

"Don't forget," Bow warned, "he who laughsh lasht laughsh lasht."

"Bow!" boomed Shum. "Wow!"

Dewey continued. "When we leaves to come, we are met in town by maybe one hundred converts who have hear some way that he are leaving."

"Goddam Chinese gathered humbly center of town," Bow said. "Goddam Chinese 'pplauded and prayed and waited for me to lead them. Wanted to follow me on this mission. I think would've been splendid have my flock following me, like crushade in days of old." He burped violently.

"Yes," said Dewey. "But he decided against that, and while he tells them they can no go, some great Navy officers come by. Their faces drop many miles, and before they gets their sense recovered, Mister Bow and I here leave town without the converts and we hides first two days in hills off the paths. Maybe the Navy doesn't want him to go, I think."

"We're going to greet the goddam fleet with valuable information," Bow said.

"Goodness," I said.

"Tell you, feel pretty safe from Japs, God bless 'em, but not from executive officers," Bow said. He took a drink, and added, "What you think I should do?

"Bow Wow!" Shum shouted.

"Have another drink," I suggested.

Shum gave him another bottle, and instead of drinking just a long one, he guzzled the entire contents with two jumps of his Adam's apple. "Bow!" I shouted. "Wow!" That was all the wine we had. I was going to tell him off when I noticed beaded sweat lines on his face and saw his eyebrows working up and down with a peculiar nervousness. He actually seemed sick, so instead of cursing, I politely asked him whether he ought not to lie down. He looked up and put his hands to his head in a vise.

"I'll never get there," he said hopelessly.

"Where?" I asked.

"Don't make fun of man whose state seems so bad," he said. "Alcohol an' I enemies during my youth. A game of tag played with the world. I lost. Joined anti-alcohol organizations to spread humanity like jam all over smiling square-and-triangular faced brethren on earth, this land the Lord gave us, and what happened? What happened?"

"I'll be goddamned if I know," I answered.

"Coursh you don't know," Bow said. "Nobody knows. I don't know. An' I once knew, when I was four years old and wisest man in world, if we could transchcribe thoughts of those truly wise men into adult calculations we would've solved every problem confrontin' man in his most noble an' pure state." He stopped and a minute later said, "I ask you are we out of the wine of the Orient, Flying Tiger Juice, liquid exshcrement of flying tigers, as some of our brethren in this part of the world would've named nasher's alcohol?"

"No," I said.

"Give it to me."

"There is no more."

"You just said there was."

"I just said there was not."

"You said no."

"Yes, but there isn't any."

"I know, I know," Bow said, and he tried to stand up. The sun was hotter. He stepped into sunlight. "And now I must fold my green tent of leaves like the Arab and try to steal away to warn the fleet that if there's one if by land and two if by air. That isn't right, is it?"

I stood up. "You'd better stay here a while," I said. "Sleep it off."

"On no," he said thickly. "Must go warn them. Get to coast by eighteenth of July in '45."

I caught him by his elbow and helped him back to the shade, where Shum and Dewey were recalling the good old days.

Bow said, "Must go."

"No," I said.

"Must go."

"You can't, Bow."

"Must go. Duty calls. Must go."

I let him fall down on the green bank.

Shum got up and stood behind me, facing Bow and Dewey. "Good idea is to get more wine. Give him more wine and soon he goes to sleep and sleeps off the drunk. I'll go to the mission with Dewey and get some."

I said go ahead, fast.

I sat down and wondered what to do to help Bow get safely to the coast. I also wondered how the hell the Navy had picked him for the job.

"Must go."

Although I was at first disgusted and disappointed because he would see the Navy before me, I felt better now, and the old confidence of vanity foresaw the Navy agent not getting to the coast at all. Shum and I would receive credit for the mainland operations.

If we got him drunk enough, it was possible to have coolies lug him back to his headquarters on a sedan chair. I thought about that for a few minutes. But it wasn't right, and besides, the Navy would get mad as hell and might try to capture me instead of the Japs. That was no good.

"Must go."

"Shut up."

"Must go."

With the help of a few of General Tong's agents and my bodyguards to go with him, Bow could conceivably get to the coast from where he could broadcast. I decided to ask the general's advice after Shum returned with the wine. I didn't have to wait long. The two interpreters returned in a few minutes. Bow fell asleep after drinking another bottle.

Shum and I went to the general's farmhouse, leaving instructions with Dewey to stay with Bow and not let him go.

General Tong was inspecting hand grenades around his house when we arrived. After we had tea and cakes, I told Tong about Bow.

"The general says he will give him four trusted bodyguards who can get him to coast because they know land from experience and not maps," Shum said. "They will keep to the hills and travel at night on paths away from towns."

"Tell General Tong we'd like to send along a couple of our bodyguards," I said.

"The general says that is fine. He asks what reason is there for men going to coast."

"There's going to be a landing," I said. What the hell, if General Tong didn't know what was coming off, who the hell should know?

"The general is highly glad. He would take him there himself but must stay here to give orders," Shum said, and then he backed away, for the general had grasped us by our arms and was laughing. "Victory is ours, the general says."

Tong snapped his fingers, a soldier came running, the

general spoke to the soldier, the soldier ran off, and in a minute three more soldiers came out.

"Sterling bodyguards, General Tong says."

The bodyguards looked like farmers, barefoot with rice-field mud caked over their ankles, wearing wide-seated coolie shorts. They stood casually in a line, their heads slightly though not respectfully bowed.

"They are ready to leave. Utmost security with them. Don't have to worry about giving Hobart Bow to Japs."

The Japanese would have given more than a million Chinese dollars for Hobart Bow; they knew it too. All the Chinese in the area knew of the bounty on my American head; I was worth $1,250,000. These bodyguards were loyal even though they never had enough to eat and all the money they received in pay from their government was used to buy rice.

"Shum ask General Tong what religion do his bodyguards belong to," I said.

"He says Buddhist, and what a goddam question."

"Tell him about Hobart Bow."

Tong laughed when Shum told him.

"General Tong say that is old story," Shum said. "Some-times he has Christian soldiers who try to convert other soldiers. Old story to him. But fun anyway. Fat old general up north who became a Baptist. Wanted his soldiers to be Baptist. He line them up on parade ground one day and tell them they all going to be Baptist. But first he got to wet. Then he water by hoses while they stand at attention. General Tong says old story. But never mind. Hobart Bow will get to coast."

We left him, returned to the mission, and chose two of our bodyguards to accompany Bow. They were eating break-fast and they got up scowling. They followed us out of town.

Bow was still sleeping. We left instructions with Dewey and wished him luck. Then we shook hands with everyone and started back to the mission.

On the way Shum shot glances over his shoulder and scratched his head frequently. "This mixes me, but what can we do?"

"Nothing," I answered. "Wait and see."

"Those men. Those men are crazy," he said decisively.

During the next few days we drew final maps of the coastal area and the placement of the Japanese with less enthusiasm, since we were no longer the only men near the landing area. Two days before the nineteenth of July we told Lung what was going to happen; he was so excited that we looked forward again to the invasion. And General Tong was bouncing to the mission every morning and afternoon to pick up what news I had heard during the day on the radio. There was no news about the fleet, certainly. There were reports, though, of a typhoon roaring near the Philippine Islands heading northward toward Formosa and the China mainland.

The day we told Lung, rain swarmed up the valley in a stiffening wind, racing for the light part of the sky in the west. In the late afternoon the rain began to fall at a sharp angle, and by the early-dark evening it had leveled off to a machine-gun force, pushing horizontally for long distances, breaking second-floor windows in the mission and sending the town-folk quietly under straw roofs that huddled defeatedly close to each other like drenched birds with shut wings.

General Tong visited us after supper. He had received reports that the American agent was perched in a house on a point on Hiechechin Bay; when he looked east from his window he saw only water, the Pacific Ocean. The general had told his agents in the area to keep him informed of the moves of the American and the bodyguards.

The general wore a dark brown garment resembling tobacco leaves shaped in the form of a tepee. Now he raised it, got under it shivering, and reappeared as two eyes and a pair of boots. The sides of the tepee rustled as he started to leave. He said he would let us know as soon as he heard anything about the men by the ocean, and he asked, as a parting favor, if I would get his son into West Point as soon as the war was ended.

There was no landing during the next couple of days. The rain kept up and moved now in strong, whipping gusts, and sometimes it seemed as though we were deep in the ocean watching the flows, twists, and currents mounting in powerful regularity. We became so used to the sound that we were no longer conscious of it and other sounds were noise. The tall palms and bamboos hooked at their peaks like lamp posts, and all the birds were hiding somewhere out of the wet wind.

The rain slackened on the twenty-first; paddy fields were inundated and young shoots floated sluggishly in rafts of debris. With the worst of the weather gone, we believed the landing would take place in a day or two. It would be fun to capture the Japanese with their feet stuck in the mud.

On the twenty-second General Tong reported that Hobart Bow and Dewey Lum had been captured two days before and the bodyguards, including our two men, had been killed. The Japanese had taken Bow and Dewey to the garrison in Haifeng. Tong had already sent about twenty guerrillas disguised as farmers to Haifeng to try to rescue them. I sent a message to headquarters, and the next day I received a message from an inland American naval command: CAN YOU GET

NAME OF COMMANDER, SERIAL NUMBER, ETC. JAP COMMANDER
AT HAIFENG AS MAY NEED SAME ON WAR ATROCITIES IF BOYS
KILLED AS RUMORED. APPRECIATE SOONEST REPLY.

General Tong came over the following morning in time
for breakfast. He smiled as usual and sat down by the table
on the balcony. As we began to eat, I noticed he was pecking
at his rice. I asked him if he felt well.

"News of sorrow," Shum said. "Japs kill Dewey Lum.
They kill Chinese right away. First thing they do is kill Chi-
nese." He seemed to be talking to himself. "Well, that's war.
Death is the custom."

I asked how he had been killed.

"Just killed," Shum answered.

"How?" I asked.

"The general's agent say yesterday morning fifty Japs lead
Dewey out to the gate of the middle school where there is a
big field. They untied his ropes and gave him a shovel. They
made him dig grave in the earth which was very muddy. Then
the Japs pushed him in the hole and he started screaming and
they stand around laughing and pushing him back down each
time he stand up and comes to sides. Then Dewey stops
screaming and a Jap threw a shovel at him and he fell down.
General Tong's agent say he was buried alive."

As the general spoke he looked steadily at me.

He stopped and Shum translated, "General Tong says
he knows how boys were captured. One of his soldiers was
not at the house when they get captured. He was on other
side of bay. He finds out from people when he hears firing
and comes back. The general says they got to coast all right,
even though it was terrible weather in the hills and sometimes could hardly move against the strong rains. They go

to an agent's house. It was on the water. They set up radio with aerial in back room but no contact because the weather was too bad. They sat and waited for weather to end. The weather didn't end, and Bow gets restless. He feels nervous and wants some wine to keep him steady. He gives the bodyguard some money to go to Lukfeng and buy some wine. He buys wine and sees on way out bottle of Jap whiskey. That will please Bow, he thinks, so he buys it. There are Japs in the store, but that doesn't worry him, for he looks like a farmer and has enough money to pay for wine and the bottle of whiskey. He hands over the money and leaves. He finds out later than the money Bow gives him is not used for a long time around Lukfeng. The next day the rain dies down but gets strong again. A little Jap steamboat that travels at night from Swatow to Hong Kong puts in because it is too dangerous on the sea. The Japs come to the bay, get off the boat, and look around for a place to stay. Two bastards walk by the house and see from window the muzzle of a gun. They call up, thinking it might be Japanese soldier's gun, but the Chinese in house come out excited, and the Japs get suspicious and go to find Jap soldiers in town.

"The general says Japs from town and from the boat meet and go to house. Bow sees them coming and throws a bottle at them from the window. Dewey fires the first shot. Then a battle begins. The Japs are victorious. The bodyguards they kill right away and take Dewey and Bow to Lukfeng. Then they go back to the steamboat and go down coast in the morning and come in later at Swabue and then march to Jap garrison at Haifeng where the Jap colonel lives. They were held with guards looking at them day and night. In the morning Dewey was led to the gate by the middle school."

I told them I was sorry to hear that, and as I spoke I had the feeling that the words, because they were obvious and unnecessary, destroyed the aspect of sincerity.

"General Tong says," Shum said, looking at the general, "in war you can expect that. Kind hearts left out in war." And then, as though he were not addressing me at all, Shum said, "The Chinese are used to that. For us it is always the same."

Shum looked at me. "You should not worry. You cannot help."

I said, "Is there something we can do to save Bow?"

Shum replied in a monotone: "Nothing. General Tong says when he first hears of capture he considers attacking the Japs swiftly at night and taking Bow away, but there are too many Japs. Then he considers maybe attacking them when they take Bow from the garrison in Haifeng. "

"Did he?"

"No. The general says that higher Japs may want to question Bow, Japs in Hong Kong and maybe in Tokyo, so he wouldn't stay in Haifeng with Jap colonel. When they take him out in morning they lead him on short winding road by the sea to Swabue. The general's guerrillas cannot attack because they don't have equipment and besides there are hardly no trees or places to hide on way to Swabue. They dressed Bow in Jap soldier's uniform and blindfolded him and marched him in the middle of the formation for fear of escape if we should try to rescue him. The Japs do a pretty good job, General Tong says."

I asked him what they did to Bow.

"The general's agent reports they take him to the steamboat with the soldiers going on the ship down the coast. They put him on ship and then went out to sea, probably going to

Hong Kong. If you get past frontline soldiers alive, General Tong says you have good chances to live, so he thinks they take Bow to Hong Kong where the Jap generals will try to get information from him. Nothing to do, you see."

There was nothing more to say, and after we had sat around the table doing nothing for ten minutes, General Tong got up, smiled automatically, and left the mission.

Spasmodically the sun came out the next few days, but on the twenty-seventh the sky was dark and the winds got stronger and gusted cleanly up the valley. "Those crazy guys," Shum said, watching the rain coming up the valley, "sure to get themselves killed. Fools. Dewey Lum didn't have the best sense when we went to school at King's College."

On the twenty-ninth the wind announced the entrance of another typhoon. The sky was dark and low and fast moving. It was the last day of the expected landing. I wanted to say something about it, but somehow I couldn't. I hoped Shum would mention it. He didn't. In the afternoon, while he and I were in the radio room for the scheduled report urging Lung not to give up, to keep on trying to contact headquarters, I thought I heard Shum say, "Must go." But I wasn't sure.

The wind screamed in the evening like a siren, and when I got into bed to go to sleep I lay awake a long time. The room was damp and spray came in often, and the lime walls had changed color and smelled cold. Listening, I was nervous and scared, thinking of rain falling on the field by the middle school.

11

SWEPT AWAY THE

DESPERADO

FROM THE third week in July until the end of the war, I lived in a small, dirty cubicle, without windows, next to the WC. Smelly as it was, it was a good hiding space.

We received a visit from General Tong one day in July. "The general," Shum said, "is surprised we do not know situation is much worser than we know." Shum and General Tong exchanged words, then Shum went on, "The general says one of his agents overhears in tea shop in Swatow that Japs are sending thirteen or fifteen special agents to get you. Japs say you send too much intelligence." He paused and said evenly, "Ha. That's a laugh." He watched for a smile on my face; I smiled. Shum continued, "They get tired of you. General

Tong says he knows who are Jap agents, but there are good reasons why they are not captured. Too many of them now. For another reason, it is cheaper, he says, to let his agents follow Jap agents they already know. Besides, the Japs have agents following the general's agents. They follow each other two times two. General Tong advises, for best luck, you stay inside. He thinks you better hide yourself. Maybe make the radio room your bedroom, and stay in it."

"You do not want to get killed," Shum said, shaking his head. "You stay inside and do not go outside. Miss Caroline waiting for you."

Miss Caroline, my girl in the States, was one of the things for which I was fighting, along with a Kelvinator and a long view from a hilltop, and she seemed to be as logical a reason as any for me to answer, "Shum, you're right. And the radio room isn't so bad."

I thanked General Tong and said goodbye to him, and after he left with his guerrilla bodyguards, I began my hibernation in the radio room. It was narrow and stone-damp; outside was the balcony and the mission's bell. I could not convince myself that there was great danger lurking outside; I stayed inside because I was lazy. Nevertheless, I slept with my .45 under my pillow, and when I went to the honey pot on the second floor I sat with the pistol on my knees.

One night I awoke to a noisy force trying to open the door at the top of the stairway that led to my bedroom. "Bastard!" I heard Shum yell. "The dark gets in my eyes!" He poked one of the bodyguards who had been sleeping on the floor near his bed on the balcony. The bodyguard jumped up and charged the door with his carbine extended like a bowsprit.

"We'll get him!" Shum howled, adding, in Chinese, expletives whose import was obvious despite my inability to curse effectively in that language. The bodyguard opened the door, ran down the stairs, and found no sign at all of the visitor.

"Maybe it was a Jap," Shum said. "Do not worry, we have many bodyguards." I muttered a monody of self-pitying *ai-yah*s and lay down on my bed.

The night after the attempted break-in, when I had been in seclusion two weeks, headquarters sent a message that they had received information that Japanese counterintelligence was looking for us. "Crazy bastard," Shum said not very excitedly. "They do not know anything. Major Fletcher. Ha!" I admitted they didn't know what we knew, but just what we did know, I was damned if I knew. I was scared after the intrusion, and the OSS "suicide pencil," a single-shot .22 that looked like a pencil, which had been merely a fascinating object to take home to show friends, gradually threatened the calm with which I regarded my adventure.

"Maybe Japs will try to kill you," he said.

"If the bastards seem sure to get me," I explained heroically in the spirit of Nathan Hale, "I want you and Lung to take off and forget you were ever with me."

Shum whistled "Taps" with profound expression.

In August, after the first atom bomb had been dropped, we received a coded message from Major Fletcher:

RE SURRENDER. NO PERSONNEL WILL ACCEPT SURRENDER OF
JAPANESE UNIT OR PERSONNEL. IN EVENT ATTEMPT MADE TO
SURRENDER, SENIOR JAPANESE OFFICER PRESENT IS TO BE
INSTRUCTED HE IS RESPONSIBLE FOR ACTION AND CONTROL
OF HIS UNITS AND THAT YOU WILL DO EVERYTHING POSSIBLE

TO HAVE HIM SURRENDER TO PROPER AUTHORITY WHICH IS
REGULAR CHINESE OR ALLIED ARMY UNITS. REASON FOR
ABOVE ACTION IS THERE MAY BE CASES WHERE LARGE UNITS
WILL ATTEMPT SURRENDER. THIS WOULD PUT US IN RESPON-
SIBLE POSITION WHICH WE UNABLE TO FULFILL. THEREFORE
DECISIVE ACTION AS ABOVE NECESSARY. NO SURRENDER WILL
BE ACCEPTED.

"What in the world?" Shum asked.

I said I didn't know.

Another message further confused us:

FROM TOPSIDE. RE POLICY ON COMMUNISTS: AMERICAN
PERSONNEL WILL TAKE SUCH ACTION AS NECESSARY TO
PROTECT AMERICAN LIVES AND PROPERTY AGAINST ANYBODY
WHETHER COMMUNISTS, NATIONALISTS, OR PROVINCIALS.
ACT ACCORDINGLY.

A few days later, while we were eating breakfast on the balcony (bodyguards conveniently guarded me, forming a port-
able and constant screen), two figures appeared on the paddy
paths on the terraced slopes heading for the mission. As they
came closer, we noticed they were dressed in sand-colored
cavalry britches. One man was uncomfortably fat, the other
unusually thin. They looked like Laurel and Hardy.

They came into the compound, stopping respectfully
when they got to the shinfoo's garden. They looked up. The
thin man bowed, the fat man tried to bow, and he succeeded
in leaning forward awkwardly. He raised his right hand to
his forehead.

Shum got up, went inside, and in a moment appeared in
the courtyard. There was the sound of gibberish, then Shum
looked up and yelled, "Japanese!"

"Ask them what they want," I said.

Shum flung his arms akimbo and began to question them. "They want to surrender. About fifty of their friends are waiting in the hills for you to let them surrender. They are from Kityang garrison. They declare they do not care for any more of war. Enough fighting. The end, they say." Shum paused. "What we do?" he asked.

"Do?" I asked.

"Do," he said.

"Tell the bastards we can't accept their surrender. We'd like to. They can give up to China."

"They don't wish to surrender to China. They want America."

"America regrets that their surrender is unacceptable. Tell them how to get to General Tong's headquarters."

The Japanese sent their fists heavenward in protestation.

"No, no!" Shum's voice rose to a high pitch. "They say they don't want to surrender to General Tong. They fear him and guerrillas."

"Tell them to go back to their garrison."

"They say thank you. Will do that. They wish you pleasant cheer."

"They must go now," I ordered.

Shum talked, and before they had a chance to reply, he turned around and came back in the mission.

The two Japanese soldiers shook their heads in amazement then left the compound, walking in single file back to the hills.

Shum came out on the balcony and sat down. After eating a bump of rice, he put down his chopsticks. A bewildered look came over his face. "Maybe they could have had some rice," he said. "I don't know."

General Tong assembled his guerrillas at a farmhouse closer to Hotien. He visited the mission frequently, sipping bitter Swatow tea in my bedroom. One evening the general wanted to know whether I thought there would soon be a landing on the China coast. "Tell General Tong I think the war will be over in a week or two," I said.

Tong smiled.

"The general says," Shum translated, "that you are wrong. The news of the atom bomb does not impress him."

"Tell him not to worry," I said confidently. "If it's over during the night, I'll fire my pistol to let him know."

After Tong left to return to his guerrillas, I went to bed, which consisted of four narrow boards resting on two horses. There was no mattress, and since the boards were somewhat warped, I must have looked like someone assembled in three parts when I got up in the morning. Such accommodations resulted in frequent insomnia, prompting nightly visits to our small but powerful radio to receive news reports. When I went to the radio that night I heard, much to my dismay, that Admiral Mountbatten had said it was folly to think the atom bomb meant a quick end to the war. I tried to find a more encouraging news broadcast from a different station but failed.

The next night I awoke around 3:15 in the morning and went to the radio. I put on the earphones and turned the dial. The first words I heard were "jubilation in Chungking." There was jubilation also in Paris and New York: the war was over. I ran out to the balcony, shouted the news to Shum and fired one round from my .45, aiming just above the silhouette of the highest mountain. Why just fire a revolver, I thought, when I could also send the news to General Tong with a merry instrument? The rope that swayed the mission's bell ran across the balcony. I began pulling on it furiously. Shum went to the radio.

Figures scurried through the street, so I rang the bell again, louder. The streets seemed to fill up in a few minutes —and just as rapidly to empty. There was a general exodus from the town, and in the fleeing crowd I noticed some of our bodyguards. Shortly after, General Tong came puffing up, grabbed the rope roughly from my hand, and stopped the bell. Shum came out on the balcony and received a torrent of words from Tong. When the general finished, Shum turned to me. "The general says ringing of bell at night is signal that bandits come to Hotien. That is why everybody runs out of town."

I sputtered an apology. There was nothing to do, I was told, nothing at all to do. The poor townsfolk would huddle overnight in the hills and return to their homes in the morning.

Father Tan appeared in the doorway of the balcony, rubbing sleep from his eyes. He came outside and spoke to Shum.

Shum grinned and said to me, "Father Tan thinks there are no bandits. He says you are drunk."

"Tell him the war's over."

Shum spoke a minute to Father Tan, who suddenly raised his hands as if to say "Enough," then grasped our hands and said to me, "Bonus filius. Malus pater."

"Non," I said. "Malus filius. Bonus pater."

Father Tan smiled and went back to bed.

The party to celebrate the end of the war was held a few nights later, by which time the frightened and frazzled residents had begun trickling back into the streets. It was held in the best tea shop, and all the leading military, government, and ecclesiastic leaders were there. An enormous number of toasts were poured; my toasts ran all the way from the generalissimo to various members of the Washington Senators. After we had got decorously drunk on rice wine, a group of ten freshly scrubbed school children, five boys and five girls, came to the tea shop accompanied by a sallow man with large ears. "You have surprise," said Shum. "The general knows you understand a little French, and that teacher"—Shum pointed to the sallow man—"knows a little French but no English. General Tong asks him to teach his pupils a cheer for you. Wait," cautioned Shum. "You will have surprise." I smiled at the children and proposed a toast to them, and when we had finished our toast, they stood behind me. The children were muttering something in a chorus which seemed to be funny to them. General Tong proposed a toast to hand grenades, and as we drank our wine at *gombei* speed, he winked at the teacher, who signaled his pupils with a wave of his hand. They burst into a victory yell. "Pas Mussolini! Pas Mussolini! Pas Hitler! Pas Hitler! Pas Hirohito! Pas Hirohito! Vive La Truman! Vive La Truman!" They stopped as suddenly as they had begun, as though the yell had been a surprise to them. "Ask them to do that again, Shum," I said. "That's wonderful!"

Shum spoke to General Tong, General Tong addressed the teacher, and the teacher spoke to his pupils. They did it again. After the second chant they wanted me to give them a song or a yell. I sang my college football song in French. Then I sang "Dixie" and "Chattanooga Choo-Choo." They cheered and clapped and asked me to sing these songs again. I did.

After another set of "Pas Hitlers," they stood behind me and muttered repetitious sounds, which seemed to occur with the regularity of a litany. The word I recognized was *mai kwok run* (American). While I was busy trying to persuade Shum to tell me what the children were saying, the officials were signing a few words in Chinese on a small folding scroll which, when it had been signed by everybody, was handed to Shum to translate into English writing. One of the more interesting ones said, "Swept away the desperado, our allied friend, Dan Pinck." General Tong wrote, "Earth is but one family to great man, my friend, honorable Dan Pinck." The shinfoo inscribed, "God give us peace with honor to Dan Pinck from over the sea." The manager of the Provincial Bank wrote, "Dan Pinck, bosom from overseas."

I nagged Shum until he told me what the children were saying. *"Kon kon ha gor mei kwok run, ian iun, da shoo ho boo gum shu lai da ma* is what they say. It means," he said, looking away, "there is that crazy American. He spends the war in a bedroom." This jolted me, for in the short time since the end of the war, I had envisioned myself a famous hero, my days in a bedroom possibly incorporated in the folklore of Southeast China. Hoping not to show dismay, I said brightly, "Shum, please tell General Tong and our other friends we'll go swimming tomorrow in the river." Shum spoke earnestly to the general, and the general frowned as he replied. "General Tong says he does not think it is safe to go swimming."

"Why?"

"Before the war there was bandit chief in this area named Lau. He taxed the generalissimo's soldiers and he knew every hiding place for a hundred miles around. His bandits outnumbered the soldiers. The generalissimo got tired of that, so he offered Lau commission in army. When food gets scarce, Lau accepts. His bandits come into army, too. Now, General Tong says, regretfully, army has no money and no food and so it has to dismiss Colonel Lau this morning. He took off this morning with his bandits; he took most of General Tong's equipment. The general is worried. He fears bandits, Communists, and provincials."

"Tell him the war's over," I said foolishly, and wild thoughts kaleidoscoped through my mind.

Shum talked to General Tong. "In fact," Shum said, "General Tong says his agents know there are goddam Japs who do not go to surrender at Waichow but come here in coolie clothes. Eighteen or twenty."

"No! Dammit, no!" I protested. Shum ignored me. "In fact," he said, "General Tong says it is good idea, and for best luck, if you stay inside until things are safe." He stopped and caught his breath.

"God, Shum! What does he think I am, a Rip Van Winkle?"

"Do not know Rip Van Winkle," said Shum, looking worriedly at General Tong.

12

JOURNEY TO

PEKING

PEKING WAS a city of magic during the first fall of peace. When I first got there I hadn't thought it was, because I was bitter at not having been sent home. The war was over, and at headquarters in Kunming the officers in charge smiled and said I had done an outstanding job under extremely adverse conditions but that they just couldn't send me home now because there were, naturally, men with more rotation points who had to return first. However, they promised that they were recommending me for a decoration. Later, I discovered that the best way for them to get medals themselves was to award them first to men who had been in the field. I thanked them for their courtesy and told them that I didn't believe I deserved a decoration. This surprised them; they kindly said they would send me anywhere I wanted to go in China. I said I wanted to go to Peking. They asked me, "Are you sure you don't want to go to Shanghai?" I told them, no, I was sure I wanted to go to Peking. All right, they agreed, the OSS had a house there and I could have a very pleasant time of it. A few days later they gave me orders to go to Peking and to wait there until I could be sent home. They were sorry they couldn't send me home, and I was bitter when I first got to Peking, but the land was beautiful and strange, and soon I thought the city was made of magic. I began walking and cycling around the different sections of the city and sometimes out beyond the walls to the clear sights of the Western Hills, looking always at new things and thinking of the old, of the China I had known and of Shum and General Tong and Charley Lau and Ha and Lung and the shinfoo and General Wu, and always thinking of Amy. But Peking was a new world, and time, as always, moved around with the half-immediate hand of memory, and the thinking of the old time gradually drew away from the memory of each day. Gradually I became aware of a curious tension in the magic of the city, completely silent and perfect, and I stopped thinking of other places, or even of home.

I arrived at Peking on a late afternoon in September. No one at the airfield knew the whereabouts of the OSS compound. There were few Americans working there, and no one I asked had even heard of the OSS being in Peking. It would have been nice if one of the members had met me, or if I had had the address of the house. I rode into town in a Chinese bus and got off at a hotel with the other men who had been on the plane and a few men riding back into town after their day's work. They were airplane mechanics and radio officers, and they griped and goddamned about five thousand Chinese between the airfield and the hotel. And smell that stink. What is it? It's shit. Like in India. It's fuel, you bastard. Naw, it's incense burning for their goddam great-great grandfathers. What it is, is Chinese wood. Old wood smells like that. I'll find me a woman who knows. Well, there weren't many Americans in Peking; Shanghai was reported to be full of every idiot, good-conducted American from India to China. All waiting for a boat to Seattle. The Americans lived in either one of two hotels in Peking, the Grand Hotel or the Wagon-Lits, and I waited around the lobby of the Wagon-Lits, watching the Americans get straightened out with the Chinese desk clerk. The clerk disappeared and returned in a minute with another clerk. When this fellow whistled, two bellhops came and got their bags. I looked around for someone who might know the location of my headquarters. A young American colonel swaggered through the lobby with a tall Chinese woman hanging on his arm. I decided not to ask him. I went outside with my cheap Hong Kong suitcase and wondered what to do.

A crew of rickshaw boys were in a huddle, laughing and hooting and poking one another. One of the boys came over to me. A tall, loose-jointed, rabbit-like creature, he must have been sixty years old. "Hi, flend," he said. "Wha you want? You just come in. You need clean Chinese girl."

"Twenty-three," I said. "Shove off. *Quadi.*"

"Ho, you must be Marx Brothers. You so funny, I laugh. See my funny face laughing."

"Ha, ha," I said. He called to the other rickshaw boys and they came over.

"Maybe you like to see good movie. *Alcatraz Island* with

Anne Sheridan. At Ta Kuan Lou Theatre is *Dracula* in Boris Karloff."

"You mean Boris Karloff in *Dracula*," I said.

"Ho, ho, ho, you so damn right. How you like Alice Faye star in *Old Chicago?*"

"Nothing doing." I was wondering just what to do, but I was in no hurry to leave.

"How you like *Grand Concert* on piano by Professor S. Maklezoffski? Sell you ticket cheap. He play swell. Grieg for two pianos. Chopin."

"No."

"You come to Café Snow. Heartiest welcome to the Allied troops coming to city. Every night at Café Snow there are dancing snakes, swing music by Duke Loo and his Philippine Jazz Band, genuine drinks, pleasant, all-time-smiling beauties, half of them dance naked. What do you say?"

"No."

"What hell you do here, general?"

"There's a war—" I was about to say "on," but of course it wasn't on, and I too very much wanted to know what I was doing in Peking.

"How about you taking me for a ride around here?" I said. "Say, around the Legation Quarter. Maybe you can show me the city." I got in the rickshaw, he got in front, did a deep-knee bend, and we were off. Before it got dark, I hoped to spot my residence.

We were part of a parade of rickshaws, passing this legation and that legation, this church and that chapel, this club and that hospital. Cypresses and cedars bordered the streets in their summer strength, independent and magnificent. We passed noble banks and small, elegant curio shops; there didn't seem to be many places I could hope to find my house. Hell, I thought, I could try the other hotel. The rickshaw boy went outside the Legation Quarter, running up Hatamen Street, beating darkness up a massive stone wall that ran the length of the Quarter. The angles of evening slowly transformed the drabness of the wall, and its stone coldness leapt outward like the highest mountain on a Cantonese watercolor scroll, solidly and without effort. A policeman stopped our line of traffic, and then, before you could say Jack Robinson, in Chinese, my boy shot ahead of the oncoming traffic and we jostled into a wider street for a few hundred yards and swept into the half-moon driveway of the Grand Hotel de Pekin. It looked like a government office building, with giant windows denoting spacious rooms with baths and telephones. Pulling to a shooting stop, I noticed a few too many Americans calling for rickshaws in the doorway; I could see more of the same inside, so I decided to run in fast, try to find out the location of the OSS compound, and get the hell out of the company of my compatriots. It was getting late, probably too late to eat at my compound, but I was determined not to eat at the Grand Hotel de Pekin.

"Wait for me," I said, jumping out of the seat.

"Yes, general. I wait here. Ask for Oliver."

Inside, the lobby was full of activity, and around the columns there were displays of cameras, jade, cloisonné, books, and vases, most of the displays under glass. A couple of grease-haired Americans were pointing at different cameras. Those bastards, I said to myself, will know nothing. Needless to ask them. "Go to hell," I told them aloud, in Chinese. "Hello, buddy," they answered. "You just get here?" Smiling, I told them again to go to hell. I went to the desk clerk and asked if he knew a private residence in which four or five Americans were living.

"Wilson Lum. Cornell grad," he answered.

"Dan Pinck. Good for you," I said.

"Yes," he said. "You like it here. You come now from Chungking?"

"Do you know the answer to my question?

"No, not know. Sorry. I am glad to help you. Maybe you come with me to my house for dinner tomorrow."

"Maybe," I said. "I've got to get squared away first. I'll let you know tomorrow morning, if that's all right."

"That's all right," he said. "I hope you can come."

"Thank you, Wilson. I'll let you know."

"Goodbye, Dan."

It was now dark outside, and firefly lights on the rolling rickshaws sped along the wide road. I went over to the rickshaw boys.

"'Lo, general," Oliver said.

"Let's go," I said in Chinese. The other fellows crowded around, laughing and slapping Oliver on his back. I got into his chariot. "Where to eat, son?" I asked. He hadn't lifted the thing yet; he turned around and recited, "Heartiest welcome to the Allied troops coming to Peking. Heavy reduction in price. Best is Ts'ui Hua Low Restaurant. A-One Class Chinese dishes in town. Chef formerly chef in Waldorf."

"Okay," I said. "Let's go there."

Up and away, around and about, we turned into Morrison Street at the first intersection, rolled down a couple of blocks, and then the front end went down. "I wait. Ask for Oliver."

I went into the restaurant. A huge love Buddha of a host shook my hand. "Heartiest welcome to the Allied troops. You one of my best American friends. I have uncles in New York and Chicago. You tell your friends about me." Three lovely but sour girls with slits in their dresses up to their thighs stood around us. "You like one. I give you private room. Everything. We wait long time for your arrival. Now we all free and show thanks for your general support in freeing old and imperial city. You pick one. Everything. They all clean. Every one a virgin. Just came from the country. Hide out during the occupation from the Japanese and Koreans, who rape all pretty girls."

I told him I didn't want a private room; neither did I want an unraped pretty girl. What I wanted was a nice, clean place where nobody spoke English. He led me to a table by the orchestra. The restaurant was not crowded, and I sensed the orchestra began playing only for my attention. Surprised to find no other Americans in the place, I looked around at the few couples who were there. They were working at their food, and no one looked very happy. Whenever I looked up at the orchestra, the conductor smiled and moved his shoulders up and down in rhythm with the squeaky jazz. Five violins, two saxophones, drums, and a piano, outshouted by an off-key trumpet. I ordered my food in Chinese, as best I could, for I was determined not to be another tourist. I made them give me chopsticks. "You been in China before the war?" the Buddha asked. "What war?" I said. He moved on, and one of the girls came over, crossing her fleshy legs as she sat down. Slim and wide-eyed, she wasn't bad looking. "Hungry?" I said. She scratched her bosom. "Fleas?" I said.

I began eating; she watched intently. "No business," I said.

"You very pretty marine," she said.

"You grow up in mission school?" I asked.

"Yes. I am Methodist believer."

"That's fine."

"How you know where I go to school?"

"Honey, all girls who speak English go to mission school."

"I go to school before war."

"You also speak Japanese?" I asked.

"Yes," she replied.

"That's good. What did you do during the occupation?"

"Secretary."

"For Japanese?"

"Only job. Besieged by unbelievable calamities."

"How many children do you have?" I asked.

"One. A girl. I like you to come to my house for supper tomorrow and I can show you her."

"Sorry," I said. "Already have an invitation tomorrow."

"You want to go to private room with me?"

"Sorry. Not now."

"You like to dance? I good at fox trot and rumba."

"Marines can do that," I said. "You ask pretty marine."

"You come here again?"

"No," I replied.

"Why not?"

"Cost too much. Too dear."

"You like your food?"

"Yes." I took out my wallet and gave her some money. "Thanks for talking to me," I said.

"You very nice," she said. "Tell me the number of your room and I come see you later tonight."

"Room 248. Wagon-Lits."

"I be there," she said. "I love you." She got up.

"I love you, too."

"Thank you."

The Buddha came over and asked me what I would like for dessert. "Real ice cream?"

"How much?" He didn't want to accept anything. "How much?" I repeated.

He figured out a sum and I gave him some paper. "This money from not here," he said.

"That's all right," I said. "It's on the gold standard. We're going to change your puppet money for it. Don't worry."

"Where you get this money?"

"Down near Hong Kong."

"What you do down near Hong Kong?" he asked.

"Sat around."

"Sitting?"

"Yes."

"Ah, you know China?"

"A little."

"That is good," he said. "I don't meet Americans who know China. I give you my card. That way you remember me. I don't like to take your money because I say this is on the house."

"I insist."

"Yes. Thank you. I go now and call your rickshaw boy."

"Yes. Ask for Oliver."

The orchestra stopped playing when I got to the door. "Hi, general. Maybe you like to go to sexy Russian girl-house. We go there."

I hopped in and told Oliver to go back to the Wagon-Lits. When we got there a party of white people in civilian clothes were standing around the desk. Maybe they're my friends, I thought. Maybe. I spoke to a gray-haired English-man in a striped European suit. Did he know of the British Army Aid Group, the BAAG, our English counterpart in Asia? They would know where the OSS house was. No, he didn't know of their group in Peking, though he suggested I might try the consulate. He had just returned from the Japanese internment camp at Weihsien.

"The British Legation, Oliver, old boy."

"Yes, general."

The British Legation was occupied by a custodian who said that he was expecting a shipment of U.S. Marines in the near future but that he himself had no knowledge of an OSS detachment in Peking. Oliver had been standing by listen-ing as I spoke to the custodian, and when I got back in the rickshaw, he said that he would take me to the house of my friends. He said he knew everything; I said I believed him.

There seemed to be a party on at the OSS quarters. I heard music and laughter, and before I knocked on the door I looked in through the French doors: there were men get-ting up to let women sit down or inviting women, European women as they were called, to get up and dance. I saw a Chi-nese general inside.

I wasn't what you would call presentable, but neverthe-less I knocked on the door. A series of knocks. Finally it was opened by a Chinese man.

"Yess, yess."

I walked into the hall with my suitcase, told him who I was, and asked him to please disturb the commanding officer.

"Yess, yess."

A fellow came out; he looked at me but didn't appear to see me for a few moments. I stared at him and remained silent.

His moustache looked like it had been pasted on his face. "Ah, my boy, so glad to see you. As you see, we are having a dinner dance this evening in honor of the mayor, you know. Awfully sorry we couldn't meet you. You understand. It took me four days to line up the orchestra. Had them come from Tientsin."

"I've already eaten," I said, breaking my silence.

"Yes, of course. Well, you see we really are filled up here. Terribly unfortunate, of course. But never mind, I've made accommodations for you at the Grand Hotel."

"Yes, yes."

"Fine. You see we have the major here tonight."

"Shall I come up here tomorrow?"

"Ah, no, ah, Pinck—that is your name, isn't it?"

I nodded.

"No. Ah, well, just keep your eyes open and if you hear anything, let us know. No work, of course. Checking and war crimes, little to do." He shook my hand, and with his other hand he grabbed my elbow and sawed my arm in what he supposed was a very diplomatic handshake. "So glad you got here. You understand. Well, fine. Goodbye. If I have to reach you, well, I know where you'll be staying. The Grand Hotel, right?"

Of course it was right, I thought.

"Ah, hem, good, you know where it is?" he asked.

"Yes, I just came from there."

"That's fine. You just retrace your route, ah . . . Pinck. Fine. Well, goodbye."

I picked up my suitcase and went outside.

Oliver grinned like a slaphappy rabbit. "What the hell are you still doing here?" I asked.

"Let's go, general," he said, putting my suitcase on board. "You so funny."

"What the hell's so funny?" I asked.

"You so mad," he said, laughing. "Try and smile, general."

"All right, you bastard."

"Now you look like you."

"Let's go." Goddam, I was mad.

"Where hell go now, general?" Oliver asked.

"You know everything. Lead the way."

"Oh, you fine man," he said with a whoop, and in a few minutes we were back at the Grand Hotel. Wilson Lum was still behind the desk.

"You can come?" he said.

"I hope so," I said. "Wilson, I'm going to stay here. Is there a reservation for me?"

"That is fine. I'll look. But never mind. I will give you one of the best rooms."

"That is fine. Thank you."

He whistled for a boy whose age was nearer eighty than fifty. I picked up my suitcase, he tried to get it from me, and I told Wilson to ask him to lead the way. I was damned if an old man was going to carry my suitcase, even though he might very well be stronger than me. Wilson seemed to be having an argument with the old man. "Tell him I'll give him a big tip anyway," I said. Then I told the man in Chinese, "You're too damn old." His geological face wrinkled; he blinked, and his eyes leaked with pleasure. Then he hit me on the back. Damn, this was getting pretty awful. Every time I was nice to someone or opened my mouth, somebody hit me on the back. I decided I would try to be a son of a bitch like every other son of a bitch. You can't lose that way.

"He has a union," Wilson explained.

"I hate unions. Thanks."

"All right."

The room was on the third floor, above a marquee and overlooking the half-moon driveway. The room was stuffy and smelled of fish and gin and old clothes. I opened the window. "Hi, general," Oliver called. I waved to him and he pointed me out to his friends. They clucked like a bunch of dumb chickens. It was still only nine o'clock, not too late to go somewhere. But where? First things first. I intended to meet really nice people; they might be Romanian or French or English, Spanish or Italian or Russian, even Czechoslovakian or Bulgarian. It is very hard to meet very nice people anywhere—especially anywhere. Where the hell are they? I certainly didn't want to yap about with a bunch of hawk-eyed, tin-plated Americans. There were just enough of them hoarding space to give the magnificent vistas a tainted air. The old Forbidden City was just up the street, on the next, interminable block, and sure as hell, they would be crowding around the sacred statues discussing the stinking baseball teams, in both leagues. Now is it reasonable, I asked myself, to come to this lovely city and find that you are shuttled off to a hotel by a fart of an American who was entertaining the mayor of Peking, a goddam lousy general, a rich general, a draftdodging rich Chinese general? Late of the war, now of a hotel in Peking, I ask you, is this reasonable? Of course not, you idiot, is what I told myself. Go bite a rickshaw tire, you dumb bastard. Don't you remember what Confucius said? No, what did Confucius say? Brother! You don't know anything. You're lucky you survived. Yes, I know all that. But how about Confucius, what did he say? I don't remember. Ha! Confucius said, and I'm sure I'm merely reminding you of this, When you are in Rome, do as the Chinese do. That's it, I said to Mr. Pinck, that's it. You're right, man. Silly that I never thought of it before. So stop crabbing about the Forbidden City, and not so many scatological references, please. Remember, Pinck, that Shum used to tell you that you cuss too much. Okay, I said. Okay.

I had noticed a bookstore in the lobby, so I decided to go down and buy a book. I tried to think of the last book I had read and couldn't remember it; probably you haven't read a book in about two years, you illiterate, monosyllabic scholar. Fact was, I remembered, I had received a copy of one of Thomas Wolfe's novels in Kunming when I had first come to China, but someone had borrowed it before I read it and the book had not been returned before I left Kunming to go out in the field. I wondered what had happened to the man who had it; the Chinese rot was too good for him. The owner was closing up in the lobby, but he said I could still buy a book if I knew what I wanted. I told him I would choose in a hurry, and while he tapped his foot, I took off the shelves a copy of *Fathers and Sons*, a fat *Forsyte Saga* on the thinnest paper one could imagine, and two cheap pamphlets printed by the *Peking Chronicle*, *A Bird's Eye View of Peking and Environs* and *Back Stage Secrets of Far East*. "Merci," the owner said when I gave him the money, thank you for dropping in. "Pas du tout," I told him, I'll look in again.

Americans of various shapes and sizes were still inspecting bargains on display around the posts in the lobby, so I went back up to my room. The room was cool and clean-smelling now, and before I got into bed I closed the window nearly all the way. There was a real sense of fall in the air. I thought of all the good things I could think of after the curious day; first of all, no work: I could spend my time any way I wanted to, no one to report to or to whom I had to give orders; I could sleep late between starched white sheets on a soft mattress; and after all, there weren't too many Americans around to spoil my time and I was certain that with Oliver's help there would be many parts of the city to explore. With luck I might meet some very nice Chinese families; perhaps Wilson Lum might become a good friend. The Chinese general mayor and all his retreating brothers could go to hell. Naturally, I warned myself, you ought to know that you must stay as far away from a uniform as you can. The Chinese who fought the war were still in the hills, fighting provincials and headquarters; they would share in one of the successes that victory brought to the rich businessmen in uniform. Those sons of bitches are the ones in the cities, accepting surrenders and giving parties for visiting American desk warriors. In this happy frame of mind, I began reading Galsworthy. This was security: Soames, that solid citizen, was a fine friend; within a generation I was a member of his family. This was sensible: Soames pleasantly introduced me to all of his friends and his antique relations. This was ten times better than *Dracula* or even Alice Faye in *Old Chicago*, not to mention a Russian girl-house. Securely and usually with dignity the Forsytes fought against the intolerant and the self-seekers. Soames, despite his great age, soon became my bosom friend from overseas, and agreeably I decided that someday I would visit him in London.

A bar of knocks on my door. It was eleven o'clock—

who the hell could that be? "Come in," I said. I put the book down. A tall and heavy Chinese man who resembled Sidney Greenstreet came in.

"Good evening, sir," he said, chuckling. "Are you satisfied?"

"Yes. This is a fine room. All set."

"I am happy to announce that I am the porter on this floor. At your service. I am called Andy by the Americans."

"Any whiskey?" I asked.

"Yes, I shall proceed to acquire you a bottle."

"Just a drink will do."

"Yes, I shall also give you some ice."

"Soda?"

"Yes, soda. Pasteurized soda. Is there any little else thing you would like now?"

"No, Andy," I said.

"Thank you, sir. If you want anything, call for Andy. Anything here or in the city."

"Yes. All right."

"Goodnight, sir."

"You'll be right back?"

"Yes, sir. Goodnight."

"Goodnight."

Hardly had I rejoined Soames when Andy interrupted us. He carried a whiskey bottle on a tray, with soda and ice; ceremoniously he padded in and put the tray on the center table. He winked at me. I was accustomed to winking Chinese, so I didn't say anything. I waited for my drink.

Andy snapped his fingers at the doorway, and I turned to see what was up. A little Chinese girl came in and stood at the foot of my bed.

"Lovely. Just lovely," Andy said.

"Christ," I said. She was ugly.

"I save her for only the highest officers, sir. She is lovely."

"Yes. She is probably Miss China. Oh, she is lovely." The woman yawned.

"You are satisfied, sir?"

"Hell, yes, now both of you get out. Please."

"You don't like her?"

"I'm sure she has a lovely soul," I replied, "but I'm reading."

"What are you reading?"

"Never mind. *Mama foo-foo*," I said.

Andy said, looking pleased, "Ha, you speak Chinese."

"You speak English," I said.

"My, indeed, yes. How long for do you want her? One hour. Two hour. Six hour."

"No hour."

"No hour. What's no hour?"

"Look," I said. "I'm busy. Some other time."

"She is ten thousand dollars."

"That is too cheap," I said. That was one way to get rid of her.

"I have others. You like to see, I go find." He spoke to the girl in Chinese and she climbed out of her Chinese suit of clothes. She was wearing BVDs, for God's sake. I burst out laughing. Of course, if she had been pretty or perhaps even not quite so impossibly ugly I would not have laughed. She reminded me of all the army sex movies I had seen. A composite of germ-carrying girls on bar stools in Baltimore.

"Oh, she is lovely," I said.

"She is very expert."

"My God, yes, yes."

"I can see you know a good woman," the porter said.

"Yes. She is much too good for me." The woman was shivering; goose pimples appeared, intermingling with other types of pimples. If a fellow slept with her, he wouldn't be allowed to go overseas with his outfit. "Tell her to put her clothes on. Tell her I got shot in the war. Otherwise I think she is a lovely girl and I think the man who could have her would indeed be favored."

Andy wouldn't give up. "She is saved only for high officers. I had her sleep with colonel last night."

That's too bad. I would never sleep with a girl who had slept with a high officer. High officers, especially colonels, are infected. I got up and led them out of my room. I locked the door and made a drink. Then I returned to Soames and England for a couple of pleasant hours and fell asleep on the way to visit one of Soames's brothers, who was still a growing boy of ninety two.

RAMBLING

IN THE MORNING I was awakened by the sunlight of civilization on my bed. Civilization was this: sunlight telling time on clean white sheets and an orange day, clear and dry and windy, traveled outside. The year had turned to fall again, the world had stopped fighting, and, after a moment's consideration of breakfast, I again fell asleep. When I woke up the second time it was past 10:00. I read a while and then got dressed and went downstairs. The dining room was closed; waiters were shuffling preparations for lunch, which would be served at 12:30. The American Army was at work somewhere, so I looked around the lobby at the different items on sale. None of them seemed great bargains; although the cameras were made by Japanese and Germans and were supposed to be great bargains (evidently higher prices had caught up with the liberating millionaires of the American Army). Probably it would be a decent thing to buy one and bring it back home for a gift for somebody, but I hated the sight of george items and charlie oboes advertising their skill and nationality, mooing about the countryside snapping pictures of one another and of insipid Chinese girls standing in the old romantic half-moon gates of the romantic whorehouse compounds. Besides, I didn't know anything about cameras. There were some cloisonné vases and salt and pepper shakers on display with a card that said where they might be bought: "39 Morrison Street, Hop Sam, Vice President, Hop Sam Company." Special 10 percent reductions to members of Allied forces. That was me. The bookstore was open, so I walked over to look. "Good morning," the proprietor said. He was dusting books on a counter. "Good morning," I said. "Fine day."

"This is a Peking day," he said. "This is the weather of the year. You do not find days like this anywhere in the world. In Paris there is a similar crust of autumn; slow motion and quiet madness; the feeling of other-whereness."

"Perhaps I see what you mean."

"You will after you are with us a few days. It is as though everything you see is through your imagination. I feel that I am a visitor in Peking during the fall, although I have lived in this city and in China for twenty-six years."

"It is lovely," I said.

"Where have you been in China?"

"All around. Mostly down near Hong Kong."

"Hong Kong? Then you must have been doing dangerous work."

"Not really. It was all a matter of sitting still. You know it wasn't really dangerous. But there did seem to be a war going on down there."

"You did pursue the war however?"

"Oh, yes."

"I hear that more Americans are coming to Peking," he said.

"I hope not."

"Have you heard this?"

"No. No, I haven't heard it. But I know we are going to start flying Nationalist troops into the city. To accept surrenders and take over the different facilities from the Japs."

"The Japanese did not respect books," he said. "They have taken the treasures from the Peking libraries to Japan. In the National Peking Library there are still some of the rare editions. For some reason the Japanese did not destroy them."

"They pursued the war very erratically," I said.

"That is the truth. Would you like to visit the libraries?"

"Yes, I'd like to very much."

"If you would give me the honor, I would gladly take you to them."

"That would be fine."

"Some day I shall invite you," he said. "Did you read in the books yet?"

"Yes. I'm in the *Forsyte Saga.*"

"Ah, that is very good."

"Yes. I've started it before. But I'm really enjoying it."

"I will have to get a replacement."

"Yes. Thanks very much," I said. "I'll see you soon. *À bientôt.*"

"Yes. I am always here."

I went through the lobby to the main door, watched the Chinese entering and leaving for a few minutes, then went outside to find a place to eat. I began walking down the driveway to the wide avenue.

"Good morning, general." My rickshaw boy came running up towing his empty rickshaw. In respect to the cooler weather he wore a beat-up gray turtleneck sweater that made him look like a 1910 waterboy. "You sleep all morning," he said.

"Yes."

"How you like China?"

"Go to hell."

"You make me funny, general. I laughing so hard."

"Twenty-three. Shove off."

He rubbed his stomach and doubled up in laughter. "Twenty-three yourself," he roared with glee. "Twenty-three! That so good. I tell all my flends to twenty-three."

I began walking again, with Oliver trotting beside me, his rickshaw on the wrong side of the street. "Where hell you go, general?" he asked.

"Know of any place where I can buy something to eat?"

"Hop in, general. I take you to French pastry shop. Very European."

"Okay," I said, "but when we get there, I won't be needing you for a while. I'm going to walk around this morning."

"Yes, general. I know you going to walk. I your flend; you my flend."

I got in the rickshaw and away we went; he passed all the rickshaws, a regular speed demon. "We go to French bakery, general. Quality and taste are our specialty." We went up the wide avenue and turned by the stone wall along the Legation Quarter, ran down the middle of Hatamen Street, and, on one wheel, we changed direction and barely missed being struck by an approaching rickshaw. We pulled up to a shop on the other side of the street. I got out, paid Oliver and told him definitely not to wait. Above the shop was a sign: "Boulangerie et Patisserie Française. Quality and Taste Are Our Specialty. French Bakery and Confectionary." I went inside: racks of Vienna and French bread, cream puffs, and chocolate eclairs. "Good morning," I said. "Do you serve coffee?" She nodded that she did not. You need a trip to the dentist, I thought. "I would like two eclairs," I said. "No, make it four." She got them for me and told me that if I liked them, she would be pleased to save some for me every day; with increasing numbers of American customers, she found it difficult to meet the demand. I paid her and thanked her.

"I here, general."

"Oh, hell." But what was the sense of walking around with bag of eclairs, looking for a cup of coffee? Lunch wasn't too far off. "All right," I said, "let's go for a ride."

We went up bright streets and narrow streets, dark streets and hugely wide avenues, by enormous walls and under arches that might have supported rainbows. Commerce was active, and I did not notice too many undernourished children. In the squares of the poorer parts of the city, within great walls, flamboyant posters with slapdash pictures of the generalissimo smiling goofily hung across the intersections, fluttering and flapping foolishly above the wheeling traffic. No one looked up or saluted and the traffic, coming from all corners, never stopped or slowed down, but rushed headlong, and like precision marchers everyone seemed to mesh into superbly, but unaccountably, functioning gear. There were many Europeans, I noticed to my surprise, looking like a permanent party of exiles; still, they seemed to be on important business or errands, secure in their movements. Not many of them were riding rickshaws. Soldiers of our Allies walked moodily in groups of two and three and stopped to try to joke with open-stall businessmen. The poor damn soldiers probably had no money and no likelihood of ever having any. They were better off when the war was on; civilians didn't give a damn for soldiers, and the businessmen might have been disgruntled after so many years of accommodating themselves to the Japanese. Their accounts had been upset, the forms of exchange were God knows what, and who knew what would come of it all. They looked very unhappy; not even the sight of an American seemed to change their composure. Japanese civilians alone walked with haste; they all looked alike, the little sons of the emperor. God damn them all. But the war is over, Mr. Pinck. Excuse me, then, God love them all. The new movement was love. At an intersection near the hotel, I noticed a lovely blonde girl pedaling across our path on her bicycle. She wore white knee socks and a tweed skirt. "Let's go after white socks," I told Oliver. "She too fast," Oliver said. Oh, hell, I thought, she's probably a German. But this will never do, son: the war is over, you have no enemy. "I get you clean Chinese girl," Oliver said. On the way back to the hotel we barely escaped crashing into an ice delivery cart drawn by a white donkey; the cart was stationary but in the middle of the street, and the owner yelled and cursed at me as we caromed off down the street, with Oliver's cursing an effective horn. He ran like hell. The trotting race ended at the hotel, and as I got out of the rickshaw, I decided to give

Oliver the eclairs. It was time for lunch inside. "I eat with my friends," he said. "After you have lunch, you see all of Peking. I show you."

Americans come, Americans go; in the following days we made singular impressions on the Chinese, and everybody turned out at the railroad station to welcome the U.S. Marines, who had come to China from Okinawa to liberate all of us suffering folks from the yoke of the Japanese aggressors. They paraded off the train and their band played their school song and they paraded hygienically by the massive Chien Men Tower and spiritedly under the archways over the great wide street. By God, here were the liberators, real, live soldiers, and the Chinese along the parade route scrutinized them with disbelief. Then they laughed and grinned and clapped their hands before going back to their all-day guzzling of tea. The Marines appeared to be puzzled during their march by the appearance of Americans in the crowd. What are they doing here? their expressions seemed to ask. After a healthful run of parading, they settled down in the American Compound and, since the British had not yet arrived to liberate the Chinese, the British Compound. For some strange reason, known only to the Marines, they were not permitted to savor the garrison life in the hotels; instead, they wore field clothes and stood at battle stations and saluted and ate lousy food cooked by their own mess men. Perhaps their innumerable colonels and generals wanted them to be in top shape in case another war broke out.

Trains were fired on; passengers fired back, and some Marines were sent on patrols northward to wipe out whatever forms of provincial aggression they met. And once a week they used to disrupt the polo field, which bordered the

Hatamen side of the Legation Quarter, and give parades for the Chinese children, during which they presented arms and saluted and awarded medals to a few unfortunate heroes who, despite a lottery full of rotation points and battle experience, had been sent to Peking to take care of the newer marines. They guarded the airfields and guarded Japanese ordnance depots and sold the inventory of Japanese war equipment to visiting U.S. Army men who had just come east to what had been a war zone, more or less. No shots had been fired in Peking in many years, the city had not been defended, and so it had remained beautiful since 1937. The Marines cleaned out the warehouse of more than a thousand Jap carbines; even small cannons were lugged about in rickshaws in daylight and sold in the sunny secrecy of hotel rooms to wheezing Army men whose job it had been to teach the Chinese how to fight. Generals were always coming and going in Peking, making speeches and giving presents and confiding to any nearby Chinese that they, the American generals, liked the Chinese people and they had many Chinese friends. The Chinese mayor-general continued to give parties and arrange surrenders of different Japanese units in and around Peking. Everybody got into the act, and anybody who was anybody in the Chinese command wore three fountain pens beneath the Order of the Propitious Clouds. The Marines marched up to their compound and the fearful Japanese came out to surrender the compound; the Marine commander merely told the Japanese officers to surrender to his sergeant major. The Marines came to North China and were kept busy accepting Japanese surrenders; fat, ineffectual reserve officers in the U.S. Army who had been with the Chinese Combat Command throughout their noncombat war (a big offensive was all set to begin in August, so boasted a visiting American general) rightfully resented their lack of a role in the sprawling, disorganized surrender parties. They began writing to congressmen and tried to get chummy with the mayor-general. Then a notice was posted in the hotel lobbies and printed in a Peking English-language newspaper:

> TO WHOM IT MAY CONCERN
> The United States Marine Corps will raise
> the American flag over the main gate of
> the American Embassy Compound at 1:30 P.M.,
> Friday, October 26, 1945. All friends of
> America are invited to attend the ceremony.
> Due to lack of space, however, only American
> citizens will be admitted to the Compound.
> No one will be admitted after 1:15 P.M.

I bicycled over to the compound on the announced day and, yes, the flag was up and the incense of beer gently wafted through the compound gate and became a grinning dragon peacefully meandering up the street, acknowledging the murmurs and stares of the unimprisoned citizens of China. In succeeding weeks fancier generals came to accept larger surrenders; some flags went up and others went down; and after the tea-party surrenders, from country town to country town, from Tientsin and Tsingtao and to Peking, and, finally, in a starry blast, the surrender of the entire Eleventh War Zone, the surrendered-to American generals would wonder, in the confines of cocktail parties, just what was the mission of the Marines in China. They accepted surrenders on behalf of the generalissimo; no Nationalist troops anywhere, and that was that. Scattered Chinese guerrillas and roaming ruffians managed to capture sections of some of the larger cities; in Tientsin, a vagabond remnant of the old warlords sneaked into the city before any other Allied group and made the Japanese surrender to them; but, later on, the Japanese had to surrender to the Marines, and the old warlord was captured and dispatched to the hills, from which point he directed short-arms fire on Marines traveling the road between Tientsin and Peking. I was not unhappy to learn of these events while reading the papers in the morning; in fact, I was quite proud of the old Marines.

In addition to the *Peking Chronicle*, the Marines sent me a news sheet to boost my morale. Then in the afternoons, I would move inconspicuously about the city, observing the Marines, checking them as they paraded and listening to them as they haggled with the Chinese merchants; mink was a favorite with them. At the officers' club and at their enlisted men's club the same jokes were told and roared over, the mob was watered by Japanese beer and Scotch, the nationality of which was unknown. The great, greater, greatest surrender was held inside the Forbidden City, on that celestial day, the tenth of October. Most of the men who had actually fought in China were forbidden to attend the ceremony, but somehow a Chinese general managed to conduct the surrender ceremony, with an assist by the visiting firemen from the U.S. Marines. The mayor-general gave a dance at the Grand Hotel that night to celebrate the fall of Japan; I picked out a beautiful Chinese girl and we danced to Strauss waltzes and Marine hymns. During an intermission I became a part of the circumference around the high Chinese officials. The old mayor-general stumbled happily around and clapped me on the back. "Winter soon!" he said. Japan had really fallen. Henry

Luce came to Peking for a visit with his editors, and during his stay at the Grand Hotel, I nodded to him in the corridor and he smiled very thoughtfully. Ogden Reid also came to see how peace was coming along, and since he and his party stayed at the Wagon-Lits, I did not nod to him. But he said during a speech that he was impressed by the manner in which the United States forces were carrying out their mission, and so I felt extremely heartened, although I did not meet him.

The Peking Lions Club and the Peking Rotary Club inaugurated their luncheon meetings at the hotels, and often they had the visiting Tientsin Rotarians and Lions in for a cheer and a roar. American bank officials also came to Peking to investigate the conduct of peace; they said that China had a great future, and since it had a great future, they intended to reopen their branches. Travelers' checks would be honored by all participating businessmen and a smart soldier would put his funds into this currency. A smart soldier would print his own money. Visiting Russians silently entered the city in American airplanes and drove to their compound in piston-knocking black sedans. Although no one else wore overcoats yet, they paraded around like wooden sightseers in thick black coats, probably searching out White Russians, and distributed to the theaters Russian movies about the war to counteract American propaganda movies like *Alcatraz* and *Dracula*. Nobody saw very much of the Red Russians; the White Russians and Eurasians one met in nightclubs were rather happy, some of them, and had visions of Russian sugar plums and caviar and a return to the homeland; others possessed an interminable sadness, and they sorrowfully watched their younger women dancing with the smartly creased Americans.

And the composite girls of China and Russia were astonishingly beautiful; tall, bronzed, and silken, they covered the bars and nightclubs like painted marionettes and danced closely with their partners, but their emotions seemed to be strung on thoughts a thousand miles away. One time I asked one of these astonishing girls to dance with me, thinking that surely it would be lovely dancing and talking with her, and when we danced she did not hear what I said but asked me if I were a marine. I said hell, no, honey.

The elder White Russians delivered milk in donkey carts in the Legation Quarter and made vodka, which they would deliver to your hotel room by the case. Like the paradoxical idea of the same concern selling coal and ice, one of them had a milk and vodka business, both put up in the same type of bottles, both equally dangerous to drink. It was hard to believe that Chinese were dying of starvation in Peking, that typhus and diphtheria were other invaders. But there were many hospitals in the city—a sufficient number, in fact, to include nearly every nationality. One day, the German hospital was taken over by the Chinese, but since it had always been called the German hospital and since the German doctors were allowed to remain free to serve the hospital, there was no real change and the Germans and the Austrians continued to patronize it. The French and English who had returned after their internment at Weihsien, Kalgan, or Shanghai recuperated at the French hospital. After the war the Germans had to register with the Allies; the Austrians, who kept their sacred distance from the Germans, formed an Austrian society to lobby for themselves. Germans of stature lived in the Allied compounds during the war; they packed up and disappeared into the hidden recesses of the Chinese sections after the invasion of the liberators. But there was no reason for them to be afraid; Americans quickly forgave them and slept with their wives and daughters.

With the arrival of more Americans, the atmosphere of a huge brothel enveloped the Grand Hotel de Peking, and a serious man would not call on a friend at any time of the day without knocking first. I wished that I had saved the pro-kits I had been given before I went to Kwangtung; I might have made a further contribution to the Allied cause. To celebrate the victory came schools of profiteers seeking compradores with gold or Americans who were willing to carry small packages to a certain store in Shanghai for a large sum of money. These were the survivors, the ones who had successfully withstood the years of Japanese occupation and were now ready and willing to cooperate and survive under a new Chinese occupation. The Japanese paid the bill for the Americans in the hotels so in the mornings for breakfast and in the evenings for dinner we would always order champagne. It was awful champagne of bogus vintage and puppet manufacture, and the men I ate with asked me if this was like all wine in China. "Goddam slopies don't know how to do anything right," one of them said. "I wish I was back home right now. Hell, Thanksgiving's a couple of weeks away."

The new Americans attended compulsory lectures given by education officers about what they should do in China. I attended one out of curiosity and heard a shovel-faced colonel explain that the men should not expect to find things the way they are at home; he used a blackboard and chalk and paper diagrams to illustrate his lecture, and when he said he was going to talk about women, everyone laughed.

"The modern Chinese girl, in her long, closely fitting

gown, her bare arms and short hair, is often very pretty," he said. "Yet it is well to remember that in China the attitude toward women is different from ours in America. Chinese women in some ways are more free than they are in America; that is, they do some things which American women don't yet do. They are in the Army, for instance, and they fought side by side with the guerrillas. But in their relations with men they haven't the same freedom as women have in America. There are Chinese girls in cabarets and places of amusement who may be used in free and easy ways. But the average Chinese girl will be insulted if you touch her, or will take you more seriously than you probably want to be taken. A mistake may cause a lot of trouble. If you get a dose, the best thing to do is see your doctor. I mean an American doctor. You may be busted in rank, but it's a lot safer than visiting a Chinese doctor.

"You all have heard what's happened to some fellows who thought they'd use a Chinese cure. And during your stay in Peking I want you all to enjoy yourselves and to remember that you are representatives of your country, and I don't want to hear of any of you fellows caught stealing pieces of sacred art in the Forbidden City or anywhere else. The Forbidden City has just been opened up for outsiders and you should consider yourselves privileged indeed to be allowed to enter it. So don't steal anything. Have fun and thank you, gentlemen!"

Sundays one might have a religious breakfast of bacon and eggs at one church and proceed to a luncheon meeting of the Officers Moral Endeavor Association and go to an afternoon tea discussion at the Peking Union Church, where Army and Marine chaplains preached on What It All Meant and Where We Were Heading. Then there were masses for German-speaking Catholics in the German chapel in the Legation Quarter or at a convent in a Chinese section. There were Methodist Youth for Christ rallies in Peking and Tientsin, in English and Chinese, and everyone was welcome to participate in the "Lively Singing and Testimonies and a Message from the Word of God." Sunday was a quiet day. Owing to the peculiar nature of my position I was able to dress as I pleased, and I dressed as a civilian much of the time. In a department store in one of the bazaars I found a brown Harris tweed suit that was in remarkably good condition, with a label that read "Julius Garfinckel, Washington and Paris." I bought a couple of white shirts and a black necktie, and I was all set to vanish from the solid comfort of army cloth and to disappear, along with about six hundred other Americans who were unaccounted for in China.

But I covered Peking on my bicycle, starting often in the mornings and stopping at Chinese curb restaurants for a bowl of rice. The Chinese looked at me with wonder when I ate my rice with their chopsticks, surprised that I did not haggle over the price. I went down narrow streets which had not seen the sun in many years, and I stopped in the shops and talked and drank tea with the owners, although they did not understand me and I did not understand them. In the European-frequented sections and stores, relations were not so friendly, and I would merely walk through in a hurry looking at the piles of clothes and displays of necessities and luxuries. Mink skins banked the counters of the clothing stores in the American-visited stores, and I considered getting a mink skin or two to give to somebody, but who wanted to take back a stinking mink? In an embroidery shop I bought two tiger skins for twenty dollars; they would be an addition to my box of trophies. I could say I shot them.

Wilson Lum had friends at a few schools, and he took me with him to meet them. The Japanese had taken over the universities, and now that the war was over the students were concerned because the new Chinese school administrators were not certain just how credits would be awarded for study under the Japanese, and the Chinese students were worried because they were certain they would lose credits, even though there were going to be general examinations. At the Peking Municipal First Middle School I became the soccer and basketball coach and had great fun kicking goals and showing off with passes behind my back and one-handed jump shots from beyond the foul line, two moves which had not yet been invented in China.

One day I went to see Peking University and, because I got misdirected, ended up at the Peking Union Medical College, where I met an American administrative officer who had been interned throughout the war. He invited me to his apartment for some coffee—Chase and Sanborn's—which he had just received from America. He was an extremely fine fellow, and he asked me if I had met Dr. J. Leighton Stuart, the president of Yenching University. He was the man I should meet, he said. And don't be surprised if the Chinese are not cordial: the student types have a mean streak of nationalism. The administrative officer and I talked about our position during the war, and he asked me whether I was considering attending medical school in America. He would be glad to help me attend his college as soon as it got going again. I thanked him and decided to visit Yenching first, although it meant a long bicycle ride outside of town.

When I got there, there was a ceremony, or at least an official function, going on; Henry Luce and his party were looking the place over, since his father had given Yenching a large sum of money. We didn't travel in the same circles. I tried to pick up a girl who was leafing through a book on the lawn. "It's pretty cold to be reading outside," I said. She looked up and smiled and I almost fell down, and then she adroitly stuck out a handful of hip as she turned around and walked away. I guessed that I gave up too soon, but I decided to return to the Grand Hotel. Back to my books. Back to the delicate flavor of my Papastrates cigarettes. Back to the delicate aroma of the Red Cross girls and the delicate dance-hall girls. Back to the serene contemplation of the great love Buddha and the wise sleeping Buddha who lies down with his hand holding up his head: wooden discomfort but ageless serenity. Back to Just Looking. Back to the old Deutsche Evangeliche Kirchengemeinde. Back to ye olde Camel Bell Gift Shoppe. Back to Soames and London.

A few days later I bought, as advertised in the English newspaper, a small 1933 Ford automobile from a prim, gray-haired man who said that he had been a general and a retired diplomat of Bulgaria. "What are you doing here?" I asked him. "What are you doing here?" he replied. I asked him whether the car needed any major repairs, and he said no, no, it will take you anywhere you want to go. That was all I wanted, I said, and thanked him. I had forgotten about the intended landing in my old war area and about Hobart Bow and Dewey Lum, then I read in a Shanghai paper, "First U.S. Steamer Arrives in Shanghai":

SHANGHAI Sept. 25

The first American cargo ship to enter Shanghai since
1938 arrived at this great coastal port on September 22
and began unloading cargo originally intended for combat operations, it was announced today. The ship, the
U.S.S. American Victory, brought many supplies including a cargo of trucks and aviation gasoline. The ship was
part of a convoy which left the United States more than
five months ago to take part in a landing operation somewhere on the China coast. . . . So there might have been
a war, somewhere on the China coast.

On an uncrowded Wednesday I decided to leave my car at
home and make a visit by train to Tientsin. On the way the
train was fired on, and my first thought was to lie down on the
floor of the coach. Since the Chinese passengers looked curiously out the windows and did not seem to feel they had to
duck whatever shots might come their way, I thought of the
honor of my country, recollected my reputation for courage,
and sat upright during the gunfire, stupidly looking outside
my window for the varmints.

It was difficult to escape from the Marines in Tientsin,
and the hotel there was also a giant brothel, inhabited by
peripatetic concubines with great sores. I met a family of
White Russians, extremely poor and forlorn, whose daughter
I had first met at a nightclub in the afternoon. I spent the
evening with them drinking tea from coffee mugs and trying
to bridge our languages with laughter and agreement at whatever was said. The daughter came back to my hotel with me
and spent the night; in the morning I returned on the train
to Peking.

"Where hell you go, general?" Oliver asked.

"To shoot camels."

Wilson Lum was at the desk. "Hi, Dan. I inquire where you are."

"I went to Tientsin, Wilson."

"Did you have a good time? I would like to visit there some time."

"Yes. I had a good time. Any mail?"

He gave me a letter which I opened immediately: How was I? Everybody was all right at home and missed me. What was I doing in Peking? Our friend Mr. Forrester had lived in Peking before the war with his family and had reported that it had been a lovely city, like Washington. What were my duties? Had I met any nice people? Was I taking care of myself? When was I coming home?.

"We got more soldiers, Dan," Wilson said.

"Damn. When's the war going to start?"

"I'm sorry but we are short of space and I have to put a man in your room with you. Lieutenant Case. I think he's a nice man. I'm sorry."

"That's all right, Wilson. Is he there now?"

"I think he is. I hope you won't mind."

"No," I said. "I'll go on up."

I went upstairs, knocked on my door, and heard "Come in."

"Hello," I said.

Lieutenant Case stood up and asked me what I wanted. "Dan Pinck," I said. "I'm glad to meet you."

"Oh. Hello. What are you doing in those clothes?"

He was searching for a rank. "General," I said. "No, really, I've clothes to fit every occasion." And I told him about my part in the war and what I had been doing in Peking. We spent the afternoon talking about Things and China, and that evening we ate together in the dining room. Afterward, with Oliver towing us, I took him to a few nightclubs. I decided, under the influence of Galsworthy, that he was a man of good will, indeed, of character. Van Case was a communications officer. He had spent his time at the airfield near Chungking; he seemed to be a pure man from Oregon who didn't like to talk about women other than his wife, who was teaching school. Since he did not refer to the Chinese as slopies and had heard of Galsworthy and Turgenev I considered myself fortunate in having him for a roommate. By nature I was not a hermit, and it was pleasant to talk without recrimination and bitterness. Van figured that he would be eligible to return home in about a month or two, and he was happy to be in Peking. When we got back to our room we had a couple of drinks and Van read *Fathers and Sons*. Since I was by now on Conrad, I read *Victory*. This was a sensible way to spend an evening.

A knock on the door.

"Who could that be?" Van said.

"Andy, probably. We'll see the nightly burlesque show."

Andy came in and bowed to us.

"Bring in two lovely damsels," I told him before he straightened up. "The kind that you save for colonels."

"What is this?" Van asked.

"A burlesque show. Don't worry. Just looking. It's an old man's entertainment."

The girls came in and I motioned them to undrape for inspection. Van crept back under the covers and stared at them.

"Awful," I said. "No bosoms."

"No nothing," Van said. "Are they whores?"

"Certainly not, my friend. They are representatives from the Peking YWCA asking us for a contribution to their building fund."

"Can they speak English?"

"Try them and see."

"Go to hell," Van told them. The whores smiled a lurid mask of tarnished gold. "Are these the ones who sleep with colonels?"

I told Andy to bring in two more lovely ladies but to leave these girls here so we could compare them. They were unsurpassingly ugly and no impure thoughts entered my mind. Andy came back with two more girls, and when they saw their naked friends they all giggled and the second team undressed. "These women," Andy said, "are passionate."

"Yes, I can see that," Van said. "They're cold."

"Those are not goose pimples," I said.

"I wondered about them," Van said.

"On the other hand," I said, "they might be."

"What a picture this would be for me to send home to my wife," Van said.

"Andy, will you please get a photographer?" I asked.

"God, no," Van said. "I was only fooling."

The girls really did look cold; I missed the old BVDs. "Well, that's enough for tonight," I said.

"Yes," Van said. "Yes, sir, it is."

"Okay, Andy, that's all for tonight."

"You do not find them to your taste, gentlemen," Andy said. "I have others."

"No, no," I said, "tomorrow night." I gave them some money for getting undressed and they smiled hideously in unison. They trooped out, with Andy shoving the last one on her rear.

"Enchanting," I said.

"Beautiful. I don't think it will be hard to be true to my wife."

"Are you true to your wife?" I asked.

"Of course I am. If you were married, you'd be too."

"I hope so."

"Well, back to reading."

"Victory," I said, and picked up my book to continue a pleasant evening's entertainment in the grand style. "I don't get up until ten, so don't wake me when you leave for the airfield in the morning."

"No, sir, general."

14

MAKING OUT

DAYS PILED into days and I continued my migration about the city. Weihsien returnees began arriving in numbers early one week, and I decided it would be a useful endeavor to try to help them. The majority of those who were in good health were put up until they made further arrangements at the College of Chinese Studies. I went out there in my car to investigate and look around. Wearing my uniform, I entered the learned buildings and volunteered. Thank you, no, but no help was needed, I was told. I told them I had a car and would be glad to drive anyone who might need to drive about, with luggage or just on errands. My efforts were appreciated but not needed. I thanked them and sadly left.

I returned to the gay and carefree existence of catering to the honorable Dan Pinck and the American personnel, and then one day in the French library, while I was looking at books, I noticed a lovely woman, also looking at books, and decided to go up to her and to volunteer my services. You can slap me down but you can't keep me down.

"Hello," I said.

"Hello," she said. So far, so good. I stood there like a grinning idiot.

"May I help you?" she said.

"You certainly can."

"What's wrong?"

"Nothing."

"Really. Why, how may I help you?" The voice was British.

"You're lovely." General Pinck, free with the compliments.

She looked slightly puzzled; but I must have been wearing an awfully innocent face, for she said, "Are all Americans like you?"

"Yes," I said. "That's it exactly. Every one of us."

There was a rare sense of well-being and I felt like a giant Love Buddha smiling down on a possible confederate. The sunlight gleamed excitedly on the roofs of dusty knowledge; it was lovely looking at books. She was narrow and blonde with wide-set blue eyes, not too tall. The hair on her shoulders was a part of the sunlight. *Ai-yah*, I felt lucky! I considered a thousand stupid things to say; making conversation was not my forte.

"Why are you smiling?" she asked.

"You're so damn lovely."

"Oh, now."

"I'm sorry. But I haven't seen anyone like you in a thousand years."

"I'm not sure if I should be flattered."

"Yes. Be flattered. It's the truth."

"Sshh. We're in a library."

"The books don't mind. They'd say the same thing. In fact, they do. All of them."

"Ah. I don't think you can read French. How would you know what these books say? You're a flatterer."

"*Mais non,*" I said. "Everyone reads French. In fact, *je parle français, n'est-ce pas?*"

"But I'm not French," she said.

"Ha. And I'm not Chinese. I'm from Peru."

"Fancy meeting a Peruvian in Peking."

"In fact," I said, "I'm the ambassador."

"Oh, so?"

"May I present my credentials?" I took out my wallet and gave her my permanent party identification card.

"My, this is impressive," she said. "I am honored to meet you."

"That's right."

"Yes."

This was straight out of John Donne's eyeballs entwining; love or lust, it was at first sight.

"And to whom does this unworthy son of Peru have the honor of speaking?"

"Mrs. Nelson."

"Mrs. Nelson," I repeated.

"Nora Nelson. I'm sorry. Formerly of Kensington. Late of Peking."

"Where does the Mrs. come in?"

"My husband is dead."

"I'm sorry." Pause, gulp and reflection. "Was he in the war?"

"He died at Weihsien."

We played Where have you been and Where are you going. Nora was interested that I had been in Kwangtung; she had been in Hong Kong before the war, although she had been north along the coast. We told each other what the war was like and what we were doing in Peking: I, nothing; she, with her young son, had returned to Peking to begin teaching at the Peking-American School when it reopened. If she didn't like it after a year, they would return to London, but first she felt she wanted to return to their home, perhaps to become oriented to the new world. I felt sorry for her and thought she had been silly not to return immediately to London, but I did not say so. Selfishly I could only think of how happy I was that she was in Peking. It seemed quite natural that she accepted my invitation to tea, that we should spend the afternoon walking, and, later, that I accepted her invitation to have dinner with her at her house.

Nora and her son were living with two elderly American spinster schoolteachers; they looked doubtfully at me until Nora explained to them that I had been in the real war. Then they politely inquired about Things in America, and we talked about the effect of the war on colleges. We had no mutual friends on the North American Continent. Nora's son, George, three years old, thought I was nice, too, so I guessed I wasn't among enemies. I read him a book after his supper and helped to put him to bed. He wanted me to kiss him goodnight, which I did, and made me promise to find him a small dog of his own before I could leave. The old ladies loved

George, and it was good to see that he was secure. Later, after some conversation, I asked their permission to take Nora out; they said I was a gentleman and, certainly, I could take her out. I thanked them and we piled out into the autumn air. We went back to my hotel and ran into Oliver. "Ho, ho, ho, general," he said when he saw us.

"What ho. Can you take us out for the evening?"

"Hop in, general. You do okay. This nice boy, lady."

We got in and couldn't have been closer together; the chill air rushed into our faces, and going up Morrison Street I kissed Nora before she knew what had happened. When she did know and did not push me out of the rickshaw, I kissed her again.

"My," she said.

"Mine."

"I won't think about it."

"Don't."

"Where did you find this rickshaw boy?" she asked.

"I didn't. He found me."

"Where did you find me?"

"I didn't. I was looking for a book and you were stealing one, so I caught you."

"Where you go, general?" Oliver asked.

"A nice quiet place, son. No cockroaches. Nice dance band. No Americans."

"Ho. Roger. Our restaurant been established here for one hundred years and is noted for its Shantung cook whose skillful cooking serves you delicious dishes. Dining rooms prepared with moderation. Well-fed ducks are well roasted in Chinese big oven. Price charged cheaply with a discount of 20 percent. Tin Fu Tang Restaurant."

"We want a dance band, Oliver."

"Ho, I go there."

"Amazing," Nora said.

"Where shall we go, Mrs. Nelson? This is your city."

Nora directed Oliver to a distant point near a city wall and stopped him in front of a darkened shop; the place she had remembered was no longer in existence. From there we went to the A-One-class restaurant where Oliver had taken me my first night in Peking. The host repeated his preamble to the virtue of American soldiers and led us to a table far from the band. Nora and I danced to an old song "played in honor of Guy Lombardo." The song did not bring tears to our eyes. A Chinese boy sang, "Is not audition I am wishing, on great big radio show / but to tells you I loves you, from coast to coast."

"Them's my sentiments," I said.

"Mine too," Nora said.

"Let's go."

"Let's go where?"

My wartime activity had been crass, but somehow I did not want to take Nora back to the hotel. It was not right. Every woman who entered those noble portals was undressed by every man in the lobby; this I did not want. Hell, I was no moralist. But there were some things one did not do. I was damned if I could think of a place to go.

We drove past the Forbidden City.

And stopped in a garden with a lake with small hills and antique trees.

"You are more beautiful than the moon and the stars on the lake," I said.

"Ah, you do know Chinese."

"What did I tell you? I'm an Old China Hand."

"Ah."

"Nice girls stay away from libraries."

"I'm not a nice girl."

"This unworthy foreign devil begs to differ," I said. There was a small hotel run by Chinese in the catacombs of the city; the Russians stayed there and that would never do. Damnation. What the hell's wrong with a rickshaw? Nothing really. Then I remembered my 1933 Ford; you could catch anything in the back seat of a small Ford, especially in China, in Peking. We went back to the hotel and got my car, and I drove to the Temple of Heaven. The name of the temple and the idea of beginning this there intrigued me.

"You are a romantic," Nora said.

"I'm not at all. I'm a realist."

"Only a romantic could make this car go. It's a relic."

"I can't help it if I can't find a good mechanic."

Like almost every sacred shrine in Peking, the Temple of Heaven was enclosed by walls, and it was closed up for the night.

"Why the dickens didn't you tell me it was closed?" I asked.

"I'm sorry."

"You should be."

"The Japanese took the key to Japan."

To hell with the Temple of Heaven. We returned to the area of insipid white men; understandably, I told myself, I did not want to go to an American-infested nightclub. We drove out in the country on a road I knew to an air field.

"The best one-armed driver in China."

"Yes, general."

Out at the airfield all was dark; everyone was snugly ensconced in their respective brothels in town. Where to go? What would Lord Jim have done in my situation? Shot himself, most probably. I laughed to throw Nora off guard. "I am not a promiscuous. . . . Oh, hell."

"Yes."

"Well, look, there's this hotel."

Yes. How could one be so lovely and agreeable; perhaps she was a blonde Chinese woman. "Did you dye your hair?" I asked.

"Quite. I dyed my eyes, too."

"I thought so."

"No false impressions."

"Nope," I said. "I'm not, as you may think, looking for anything. I think I've just found; you know what I mean."

"I know what you mean."

An attack of virtue seized me. The mechanics of the affair were too damn complicated. I strived to think of an honorable place. Out beyond Yenching in two cups of the Western Hills two honorable temples might be open: the Temple of the Azure Clouds and, nearer to the city, the Temple of the Sleeping Buddha. They might be, but, hell, most likely they weren't: so sorry. Buddha sleeping. Allied personnel come back tomorrow. Open from ten to four. All welcome. Bullshit.

"Nora, how would you like to go up to the Great Wall tomorrow?"

"The Great Wall!"

"Yes. I haven't seen it. I think it would be fun."

Nora wrapped herself in a moment of thought: perhaps she had a madman with her. I couldn't blame her for suspecting as much. "We could leave early in the morning, it's only about forty miles. We could take a picnic, put everything we need in the car—"

"Car!" She looked at me incredulously. "You weren't thinking of driving there? My God."

"Look, dear, there's a road that goes almost all the way, and there's a train we can meet not far from the Wall. I've been thinking of going up there anyway."

"Now, really," she said.

"Stop saying now really."

"Well, it wouldn't be safe."

Unsafe? The car or bandits? I wondered. It was unsafe, but you had to take chances. The war was over; you had to look for unsafety.

"Of course it would be safe. People go up there every day. Why I bet Henry Luce took a picture of himself looking fearlessly into Manchuria. Of course it's safe."

"There are bandits, you know."

"There are no bandits," I said. "There is nothing for them to rob that way. There are no marines."

"I don't see how we could go for the entire day."

"We can ask the Misses Eakin and Gudger to come along. I'm sure they won't go, and when they refuse they'll tell us to go ahead, enjoy ourselves, have fun. We can bring George back a souvenir."

"What could we bring George?" Nora asked.

"Well, we could bring George a piece of the wall."

"A piece of the wall!"

"Yes. Haven't you heard how America is slowly losing its monuments? Sightseers chip them away. That's how you are losing Hadrian's Wall, too. You chip also."

"Oh, now."

"Stop saying 'Oh, now.' Don't you think George would like to have a piece of rock on his bureau to show to his friends when you return to England? Not many boys in the world have a piece of the Great Wall of China." I convinced myself. "Really, Nora."

"You are wonderful, Dan."

"Thank you. You, too. That's what all the girls say."

"Chinese girls."

"Bosh, Nora."

We went to her house; George and the old ladies were sleeping, so Nora and I tiptoed and whispered about plans for the morning and then I left, still suffering from my attack of virtue. I wondered if she would really come to the Great Wall. I wondered if we would get there. But better there than here. Maybe there would be a Great Wall Hotel. I went to the American Embassy Compound and bought from a youthful marine officer two unused Jap carbines and enough ammunition to shoot and kill seventy-five bandits, communists, or provincials, if they had them up there. Then I gathered a supply of gasoline in tins and loaded them in my car. I went to old Tivonenko's liquor emporium and got two bottles of Tivonenko's genuine vodka and a bottle of lousy Japanese champagne. I was all set.

Van was reading purely when I got back. "What the hell are you looking so cheerful about?" he asked.

"Do I look cheerful?" I replied.

"You look like ten thousand friends of mine. All Chinese."

"Never mind."

"Are you going home?"

"Perish the thought, buddy. Nothing so bad as that."

"You've been riding your bicycle too much."

"Nothing doing. Had the burlesque show yet?"

"No."

"Well, well. Must have been a full house tonight. The truth is, I've found me a lovely, lovely girl."

"The friendly type?"

"Yes," I said. "She likes only me. We just returned from the Temple of Heaven, old boy."

"What the hell did you do there?"

"Now what do you think any honorable man would do at the Temple of Heaven?"

"Pray."

"Buddy, you are right."

"What does she do for a living?"

"That is personal. But I'll tell you. She's a schoolteacher. Her name is Nora."

"Nora what? Wang?"

"Now, son," I said, "I thought you were being true to your missus out there in Oregon. I guess I wrong."

"Do you want to bring her up here?" he asked.

"No, no. I wouldn't bring her into this goddam hotel."

"Afraid Andy might give her a job?"

"Son, she is English, she is a widow with a boy named George, she was interned during the war, and, needless to say, she is in love with me and I with her. This is a real civilian affair."

Van whistled. "I am impressed, Dan. Where did you meet her?"

"Library. The French Library."

"If I weren't—"

"Yes, I know all that. But you'd better stay away from libraries. I'll get your books for you. Want me to add a testimonial in your next letter home?"

"A schoolteacher," the poor fellow said.

"I'll probably marry her. She has blue eyes."

"I hope so," Van said. "I'll be best man."

"We're going on our honeymoon tomorrow."

"Tientsin?"

"Tientsin, hell. We're going to a romantic refuge of emperors and robbers. The Great Wall."

"I don't think it's safe to go there. If you get there."

"Come, come. What's a little danger to an American?"

I got up early in the morning and had breakfast in the dining room with Van and a couple of crewmen from a plane I had been on. They talked about the women they had lined up for the evening. They asked me if I would like to go with them, but I told them no, I already had a date. I ordered two more bottles of champagne unopened from the waiter; he smartly brought them out from the kitchen in a paper bag. Then I told Van goodbye and went out to my Ford.

"Where hell you go, general?" It was Oliver. "Don't you ever sleep? Roger, general." Goddam your roger, I thought. Goodbye. Twenty-three.

Nora was ready to leave when I got to her house. George was up; he certainly did not appear to have suffered from the war; all he wanted was love. Which is what I and the whole world wanted. I promised the Misses Eakin and Gudger that I would return early, and Nora assured them that she would be all right. What were they afraid of, me? We got in the car and I accelerated the engine fast so that the old ladies would see what a fine car this was. A spume of fuel-smoke shot out the rear. When we turned the corner I stopped the car in front of some country's legation and we kissed each other good morning. Then we drove out of the Quarter and I gunned it around the turns at Coal Hill; the Chinese flew out of my way like chickens. By the Drum Tower and then beyond the city wall and into the countryside. We stopped at a main-street town about ten miles out of the city and we opened the champagne. I had brought two little jasper cups, but they were too small for champagne. I drank first. This is the first time I've ever drunk champagne from a bottle, I thought. Is it good? It's rotten, it's not that bad, it's still cool. After we started up again, it began to drizzle, but the clouds were not low and we could see the advance of the hills and mountains ahead of us.

"Have you been there before?" I asked Nora. She told me she had. "Well, tell me if I go wrong."

"I will."

"I can't miss it?" No, you can't, I thought. The best one-armed driver in China. Amy popped into my mind: another woman I thought of bringing home. She said I was a play-boy. The hell with you, you screeching doll.

The rain spattered on the windshield, and I slowed down. There was no sense hurrying; we had a long day ahead of us, and the soft shoulders looked very soft. Occasionally strangely prosperous pedestrians strode by the roadside and farmers walked beside donkey carts loaded with vegetables and wood. Talk of love and cabbages. We reached a town at the foot of the mountains and parked the car by the railroad station. No bandits in sight. I put the carbines under the back seat and we walked about until the train came. We got on the second of two coaches, and after a few minutes we pushed on. Up into the wide giants and then coming out of a tunnel we saw the wall, the Great Wall. O Great and mighty wall, are you speechless? Yes. Properly so, scroll of history.

The country was rough, and the mountains now appeared bare and gray-brown, dipping and rising like giant waves in every direction. The train stopped for air and we got off at the Great Wall Station. The rain snapped at us; it was cold. Foreigners, we bundled as we walked. We went up a sentry tower that must have been made for tourists since the year one. And there we were. There we were. Atop the wide dragon. Old as man's history. Crumbly bastard, isn't it? I thought. But it was built by different contractors. Silent, upon a peak in Darien . . . they looked at each other with a wild surmise. I'm not totally ignorant, teacher. Please don't go so near the edge. Don't worry. I could build one of these walls for you. Please do. Do you suppose we're the first lovers to kiss on the Great Wall? What *are* you doing? Here's a piece of the Great Wall—think of that. I shall. Don't lose it. I never will.

They say that in the ancient times a signal could travel from one end to the other in less than a day. The Chinese invented telephones, too: a soldier in a sentry tower would yell or shoot his gun (after the invention of gunpowder), and the signal would be passed along that way. I love you.

I'm listening. I love you. We reached another sentry tower and jumped over a crevasse. It is cold. No, it's lovely, it's winter. Almost: it's love. Then we returned to the station and ate our lunch beside a coal fire. I gave the vodka to the station master. What does he say, Nora? He says that he hopes you have the peace of heaven and that all our children will always love us until the Great Wall crumbles.

The train stumbled into the station and we got on. Farewell, Great Wall, old friend. Then we were off, heading back to Peking. My Ford started up without a fight, and driving away we stopped to look at the mountains. The dragon of rain had devoured them. It was dusk when we reached the main-street town, and from there we saw the fortress of Peking, rising like an island in the sea. Then we came upon a camel caravan. We stopped to watch them as they prepared to follow an ageless route toward an impossible horizon.

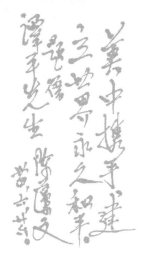

AFTERWORD:

THEN AND NOW

IN HER introduction to the Modern Library edition of her novel *Mrs. Dalloway*, published in 1928, Virginia Woolf wrote, "It is difficult—perhaps impossible—for a writer to say anything about his own work. All he has to say has been said as fully and as well as he can in the body of the book itself. If he has failed to make his meaning clear there it is scarcely likely that he will succeed in some few pages of preface or postscript." Woolf is absolutely right; and I do not intend to reinvent or reinterpret any of my experiences during the war, or to amend them in any way. Woolf also wrote, "It is true that the author can if he wishes tell us something about himself and his life which is not in his book." On that tack I'll proceed. Thank you, Mrs. Woolf.

Whenever I've been a participant in discussions with leading scholars and others who either have or claim to have profound knowledge about China's conduct during the war, my comments have tended to fade away into silence or mumbled profanities. I tell you this truly: some of our most prominent scholars, a few of whom I knew during my service at Harvard University, believe that Chairman Mao was an agrarian reformer. I never have a polite response to such a wrongheaded assumption. On occasion I have said, "I don't think that you can call a man who has killed more than fifty million of his own people an agrarian reformer." At this, colleagues and fellow participants glare at me, as if to say, "What do you know about China?"

In such settings, I cannot invoke the aid of a doctorate in East Asian studies or a list of published scholarly books. "Well, I was there," I have sometimes said. Occasionally, when provoked, I've borrowed Pearl Buck's warning, and said, as she did, "There are no experts on China, only varying degrees of ignorance." A pretty bold statement from an amateur.

There are some who tell me that *we* lost China, meaning Nationalist China. To this, I have said, "We didn't lose China; the Chinese lost China."

The question to ask those who totally castigate Chiang Kai-shek is, Whom should we have assisted in China? No one? The Communists? Or Chiang Kai-shek? Not for a moment do I think that Chiang is blameless, but as the wartime leader he was far superior to any alternative. And as for the notion that Mao was actually fighting the Japanese, nothing can be further from the truth. One of the major broadsides against Chiang is that he ran a corrupt government. Very likely he did. But he was fighting a war—a War of Resistance, as the Nationalist government called it. He was also fighting a war on at least three other fronts, including the rapscallion members of his wife's family, the Soongs, and the warlords who maintained their contrary enclaves throughout the war. The Communists tried to persuade him to surrender —that's another story. And we forget, if we ever knew, that the French government (Vichy style) allowed the Japanese to send troops into China from French Indochina.

China was at war for fourteen years, beginning on 18 September 1931, when, in what is known as the Manchurian incident, two hundred thousand Japanese troops invaded Manchuria, a province of China. This was followed by the Marco Polo Bridge incident, on 7 July 1937, when the Japanese invaded China proper. Japan surrendered on 3 September 1945. The Japanese killed roughly 16 million Chinese civilians and slightly fewer than 2 million military personnel. At the height of the war, Japan had roughly 2.3 million men in China. (Even if the war in China is considered a diversion from the main war in the Pacific, this was an asset to us, since the bulk of the Japanese troops in China were not fighting in the Pacific in the early years of the war.)

Aiming to maintain my status as a glorious amateur, the term Gen. William J. Donovan used to describe the men and women who served in the Office of Strategic Services, I traveled over as much of China as any ten Americans and I learned a lot about what China did and did not do. But let's leave the war.

When I'm puzzled, as I sometimes am, by my survival and my randomly surreal and successful leadership of our group during the war, I need only remember that all of it was due to my interpreter Shum Hay's skill at everything he did.

When I returned home to Bethesda, Maryland, after the war, I immediately went back to school at Washington and Lee University in Virginia. Although I subsisted on the GI bill, which included full tuition plus, as I recall, not much more than fifty dollars a month, I sent Shum a portion of this amount to help support him at Lingnan University Medical School in Canton. In a letter, Shum told me that he was eating less well at school than we did during the war. He ate one meal a day, in fact. When he graduated in 1948, he immediately returned to Hong Kong, having no use for the nearly triumphant Communists or for Chiang. When the war started in earnest and the Japanese invaded Hong Kong, Shum's family of thirteen—his mother and father, uncles, aunts, and cousins—left for the mainland. He never saw many of them again.

With his medical degree, he expected to practice medicine in Hong Kong, but the British, who reoccupied Hong Kong a few days after the Japanese surrender, did not honor his medical education and refused to let him practice. Instead, Shum worked as a medical technician. In the mid-1950s, he went to London and worked as an assistant to Sir Alexander Fleming, the discoverer of penicillin. With this experience, Shum returned to Hong Kong after six years and the British finally allowed him to practice medicine. He became a leading practitioner in Hong Kong; in fact, he became chief of pathology in the Hong Kong government's medical service. During the Vietnam War he had the onerous responsibility to look at and quickly examine dead Americans being flown back to the United States in their military coffins.

We corresponded over the years, and my wife, Joan, and I keenly followed the news he sent us about his family and himself. We seldom, if ever, mentioned the war. We didn't need to and we didn't want to. At one point, maybe twenty-five years ago, he told us that our radio operator, Lung, had died in Canton, where he operated a radio repair shop. Shum's two sons, David and Daniel, finished graduate school in Canada, David with a medical degree and Daniel with a doctorate in biology.

Then, in 1982, Shum and his son David visited us in Boston. Shum had flown to London, Ontario, where David did research at the medical school. We spent several days together at my house. David wanted me to talk about his dad's experiences in China. I did. I pulled out a lot of memorabilia from various hiding places in our house: Japanese swords and a Japanese rifle, maps, copies of messages we sent and received, scrolls from Chinese leaders honoring me, and other things that a professional pack rat collected. With a light touch, I told him about our adventures. David was pleased to hear me talk about the war. He said that his dad had never mentioned any of the experiences I related.

One evening, when they were alone, Shum asked Joan to tell me not to talk about the war in such a relatively jocular manner. For him, he said to Joan, the war was not a topic he cared to hear about. For him, the war was a severe dislocation of many of the people he cared for; it was not an occasion that could be recalled with mild pleasantries. Many family members and friends had been killed, and the lives of those who survived the war had been devastatingly disrupted. My memory of the war as a rather benign adventure did not match his memory of the war. When Joan told me of Shum's feelings, I stopped talking about the war as a grand adventure.

Two months later, David called to say that Shum had

died in Hong Kong. Joan said that Shum was likely terminally ill when he came to see us; he knew it and didn't tell us.

Several years later, Joan and I were in South Asia on a consulting job. On our return trip, we decided not to just change planes in Hong Kong but to stop there for a few days and travel by train for a week in Guangzhou. When we arrived at the train station and I had to arrange for a taxi to the New Victory Hotel on Shamian Island, I discovered that my knowledge of the Chinese language returned immediately. This rather shocked us. We met many young and older people during our stay. A surprising number of them knew about America's helping role in China during the Second World War, far more than we customarily find in our country. Their knowledge came from stories handed down by parents and grandparents. Almost every time we left our hotel, we were followed by ten to forty people. They considered me a hero. I didn't complain.

China is never far from my thoughts. I attribute my varied careers at least in part to my life in wartime China. For instance, I've pursued many endeavors in which I've had no expertise, or even prior knowledge, much as I did in China: serving on a curriculum content committee at the Massachusetts Institute of Technology (I doubt that I could have passed any course in engineering, science, or mathematics at the institute), teaching design courses at an architecture school (I've never had a single course in architecture), working as a consultant in urban planning (no professional or educational background), and so on. In fact, when I've been asked to engage in professions in which I might have some competence, I've turned down the opportunity more often than I've taken it. One of those occasions was when, in the early 1950s, the Central Intelligence Agency asked me if I would return on a secret mission to China. I politely and wisely said no. Had I gone, I would probably have been a prisoner for twenty years, which is what happened to two CIA agents who volunteered for a mission to help the Chinese overthrow the Communist government. That sounds preposterous—and it was—but it's true.

I did not achieve one of my main wartime goals: I never became a certified hero. And I was not awarded a decoration —at least not immediately. It took forty-one years before I received a decoration. Here's what happened. In 1986, the mailman on our street delivered a small package. It had been sent from Taiwan. I opened it and found a handsome medal in a bright green leather case. A letter to me from an official of the government of the Republic of China read, "The Government takes pleasure in sending you herewith a China War Memorial Medal which the Government of the Republic of China has especially decreed as a token of its appreciation for the contributions made by a few persons like your good self to our joint effort in the China theater during World War II."

ABOUT THE AUTHOR

DAN PINCK lives in Cambridge, Massachusetts. He attended Sidwell Friends School in Washington, D.C., and Washington and Lee University. Now a consultant, he worked in administration at the Massachusetts Institute of Technology and in research at Harvard and consulted in development and planning in fourteen African nations.

Pinck was a longtime contributor to *Encounter* and *The American Scholar*. Many of his articles, essays, and reviews have appeared in leading magazines and newspapers, including *The New Republic*, *Foreign Intelligence Literary Scene*, *Financial Times*, and *The Boston Globe*. In the late 1940s he worked as a legman for A. J. Liebling at *The New Yorker*. His most recent book is *Stalking the History of the Office of Strategic Services: An OSS Bibliography*, in collaboration with his son, Charles T. Pinck.